EXPERT COMPANIONS

OUTDOOR

SKILLS AND TIPS

EXPERT COMPANIONS

OUTDOOR

SKILLS AND TIPS

A GUIDE FOR THE MODERN ADVENTURER

THUNDER BAY
P·R·E·S·S
San Diego, California

CONTENTS

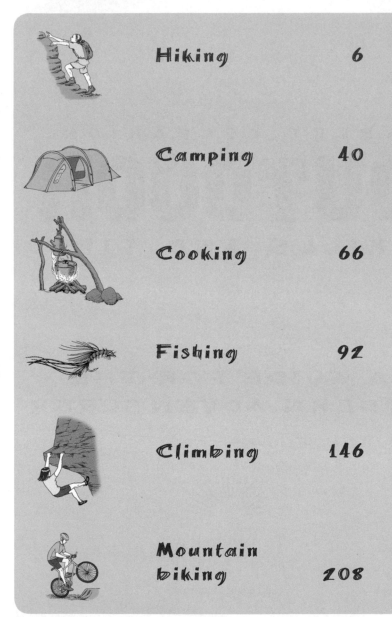

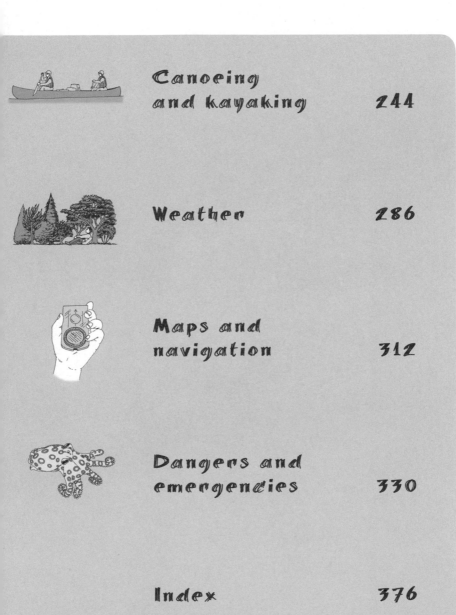

HIKING

Hiking in the open air is the original outdoor activity—it's what we humans were meant to do. It's great for the mind, body, and soul, and it will take you to places of great beauty that cannot be reached any other way.

BACKPACKS

Backpacks for all terrains For anything longer than a short walk in the woods, you're going to need a comfortable backpack.

Internal frame backpack
The vast majority of backpacks sold today are of the internal frame type, which offer excellent freedom of movement. They are typically built around two vertical aluminum staves and a rigid plastic sheet.

water reservoir

shoulder harness

pocket

sternum strap

hipbelt

compression straps

side release buckle

back pocket

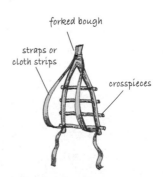

forked bough

straps or
cloth strips

crosspieces

Daypack Leave your big pack at home and grab a daypack for one-day hikes.

External frame pack These rigid, heavy packs are now a rare sight in the wilderness.

Emergency pack Tie essential baggage to this improvised pack.

MAKE A HORSESHOE-TYPE PACK

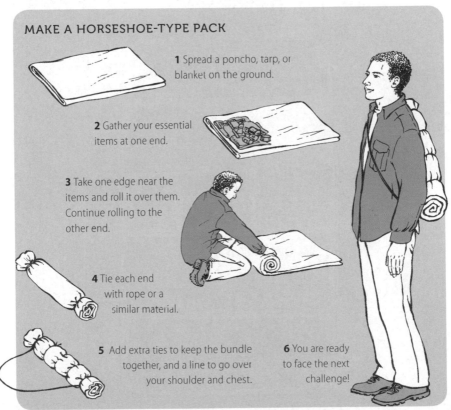

1 Spread a poncho, tarp, or blanket on the ground.

2 Gather your essential items at one end.

3 Take one edge near the items and roll it over them. Continue rolling to the other end.

4 Tie each end with rope or a similar material.

5 Add extra ties to keep the bundle together, and a line to go over your shoulder and chest.

6 You are ready to face the next challenge!

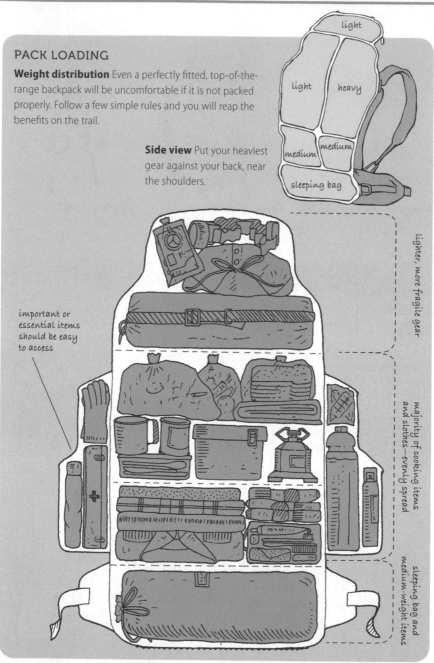

PACK LOADING

Weight distribution Even a perfectly fitted, top-of-the-range backpack will be uncomfortable if it is not packed properly. Follow a few simple rules and you will reap the benefits on the trail.

Side view Put your heaviest gear against your back, near the shoulders.

light

light   heavy

medium   medium

sleeping bag

important or essential items should be easy to access

lighter, more fragile gear

majority of cooking items and clothes—evenly spread

sleeping bag and medium-weight items

STRAPS & BUCKLES

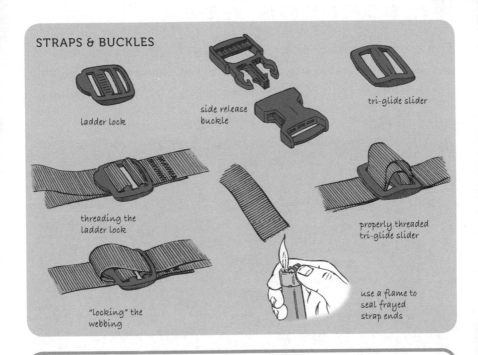

ladder lock

side release
buckle

tri-glide slider

threading the
ladder lock

properly threaded
tri-glide slider

"locking" the
webbing

use a flame to
seal frayed
strap ends

HOW TO PUT ON A PACK

1 Keeping your back straight, bend your knee and lift the pack onto it.

2 Bend low. Swivel your body and poke your arm through the shoulder strap.

3 Put your other arm through the shoulder strap on the other side.

4 Fasten the waist harness, and adjust the shoulder straps if required.

WILDERNESS GEAR

The essentials What to pack for a trip into the wild is partly a matter of personal preference and partly dictated by the environment. But there are a few items that are essentials for any adventure.

WHAT TO PACK

food

camping stove

eating utensils

lighter

cup

first aid kit

water bottle

camera in
plastic bag

cooking pot

toiletries

maps and
compass

headlamp with
spare batteries

insect repellent

waterproof
jacket

gloves

survival kit
(see opposite)

sleeping bag
and mat

clothes

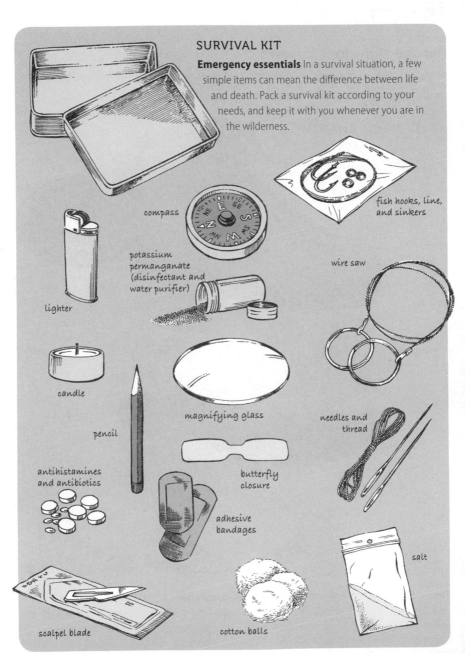

SURVIVAL KIT

Emergency essentials In a survival situation, a few simple items can mean the difference between life and death. Pack a survival kit according to your needs, and keep it with you whenever you are in the wilderness.

fish hooks, line, and sinkers

compass

potassium permanganate (disinfectant and water purifier)

wire saw

lighter

candle

pencil

magnifying glass

needles and thread

antihistamines and antibiotics

butterfly closure

adhesive bandages

salt

scalpel blade

cotton balls

13

Boots

Put the right foot forward Choose your boots carefully—they must be comfortable and appropriate for your planned activities. Always break in new boots before hitting the trail.

HIKING BOOT ANATOMY

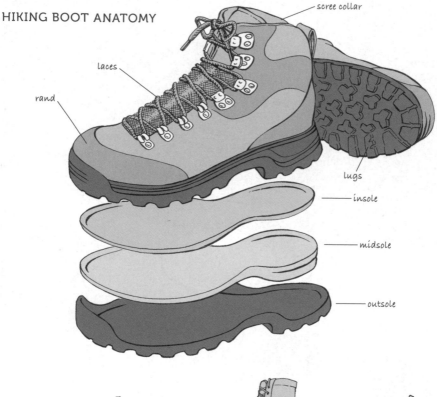

- scree collar
- laces
- rand
- lugs
- insole
- midsole
- outsole

Sneaker These light shoes are sufficient for gentle terrain and won't tear up the earth.

Mountaineering boot These stiff, insulated boots are not good for regular hiking.

Jungle boot These canvas and rubber boots are designed to quickly drain moisture.

Desert boot Suede desert boots allow the feet to breathe, while keeping hot sand out.

LACING STYLES

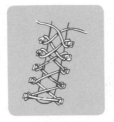

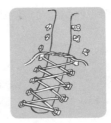

Skip lacing Skip a pair of lacing anchors to relieve pressure over a section.

Mountaineer's lace Go over and around the hook to maintain even tension.

Double hitch Add tension with a double hitch and skipped eyelets for a custom fit.

Double wrap Allows the upper area to be tighter or looser than the lower area.

BOOTS THROUGH HISTORY

Viking leather boot, ca. 900

Hessian boot, ca. 1820

medieval greave and sabaton, ca. 1400

Ötzi the Iceman's boot, ca. 3255 BC

Inuit sealskin boot, ca. 10,000 BC–today

LACING ANCHORS

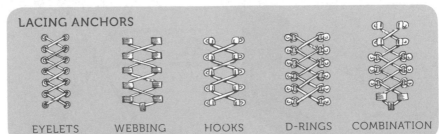

EYELETS　　WEBBING　　HOOKS　　D-RINGS　　COMBINATION

BOOT CARE

Wash After a hike, begin by washing the mud and dirt off with water and a soft brush.

Dry Allow the boots to dry but keep them away from direct heat from the sun or a fire.

Treat When the boots are dry, apply a waterproofing or leather nourishing compound.

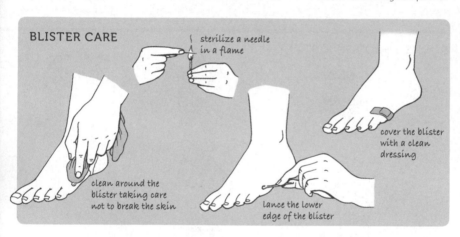

BLISTER CARE

sterilize a needle in a flame

clean around the blister taking care not to break the skin

lance the lower edge of the blister

cover the blister with a clean dressing

SOCKS

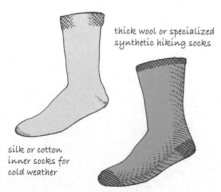

thick wool or specialized synthetic hiking socks

silk or cotton inner socks for cold weather

TREKKING POLES

over rugged terrain, trekking poles can greatly reduce effort and wear on the knees

TRAILBLAZING

Signs in the wild Keep an eye out for trail blazes and you won't take a wrong turn. If you're a pioneering type, blaze a trail yourself!

STANDARD SIGNS

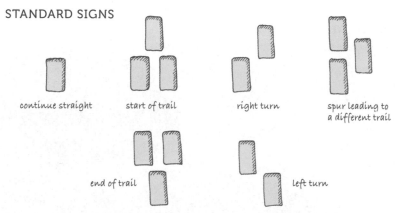

continue straight   start of trail   right turn   spur leading to a different trail

end of trail   left turn

NATIVE AMERICAN SIGNS

Look closely For centuries, the native peoples of North America have left markers for their companions to follow.

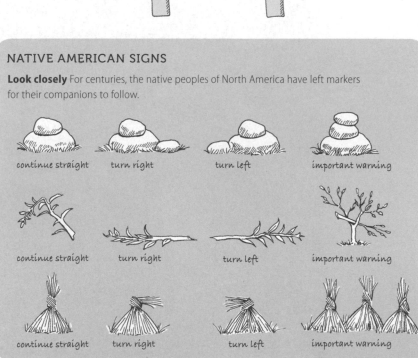

continue straight   turn right   turn left   important warning

continue straight   turn right   turn left   important warning

continue straight   turn right   turn left   important warning

JUNGLE TRAVEL

A sticky situation Jungle travel can be tough—heat, oppressive humidity, biting insects, and thick vegetation will quickly defeat the will of the unprepared.

JUNGLE STRATA

emergent layer

canopy layer

understory layer

immature layer

herb layer

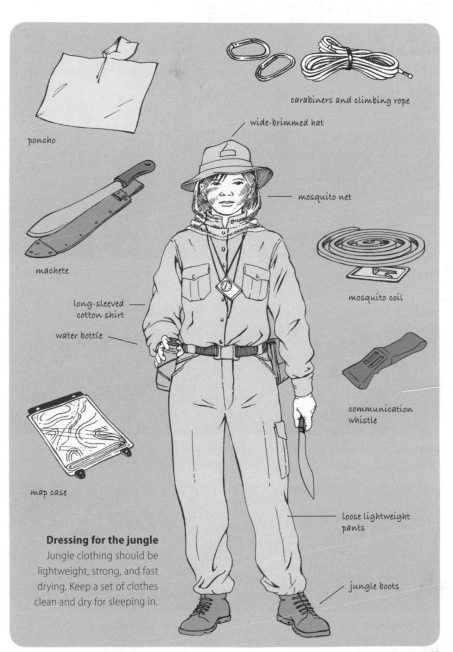

carabiners and climbing rope

wide-brimmed hat

poncho

mosquito net

machete

mosquito coil

long-sleeved
cotton shirt

water bottle

communication
whistle

map case

loose lightweight
pants

Dressing for the jungle
Jungle clothing should be
lightweight, strong, and fast
drying. Keep a set of clothes
clean and dry for sleeping in.

jungle boots

DESERT TRAVEL

Arid adventures A desert will form anywhere that regularly receives less than ten inches of rain a year. They are places of climate extremes—often very hot by day and extremely cold at night.

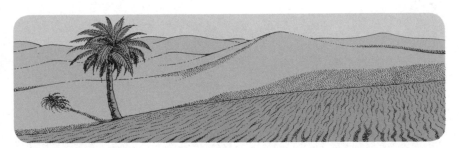

Sandy desert Also known as dune deserts or ergs, sandy deserts are extensive, relatively flat areas covered with wind-swept sand.

Rocky desert In some desert regions, the action of wind or intermittent water removes sand and other fine particles, leaving a landscape of bare boulders and "sidewalks" of smaller rocks.

Mountain desert These deserts are made up of barren hills or mountains, often separated by flat basins. Mountain deserts high above sea level can be extremely cold.

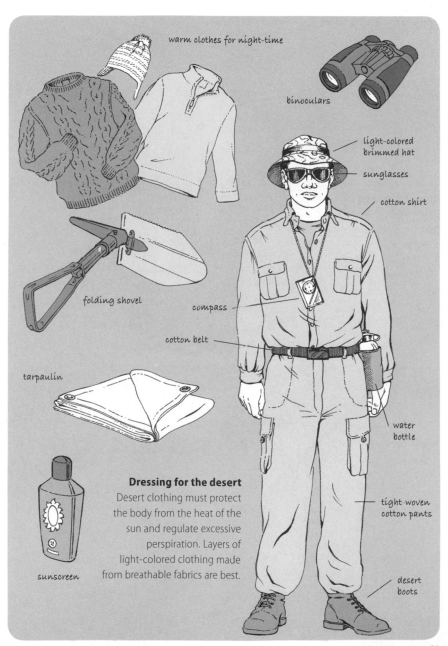

warm clothes for night-time

binoculars

light-colored brimmed hat

sunglasses

cotton shirt

folding shovel

compass

cotton belt

tarpaulin

water bottle

Dressing for the desert
Desert clothing must protect the body from the heat of the sun and regulate excessive perspiration. Layers of light-colored clothing made from breathable fabrics are best.

sunscreen

tight woven cotton pants

desert boots

SOURCES OF HEAT

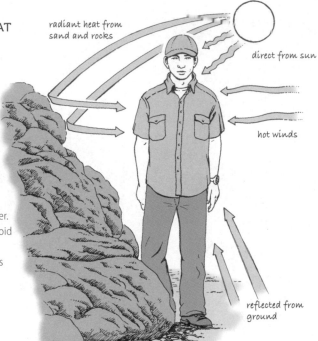

radiant heat from sand and rocks

direct from sun

hot winds

reflected from ground

Heat and the body
Desert heat can be a killer. To prevent problems, avoid strenuous exercise, stay hydrated, keep salt levels up, and protect yourself from all sources of heat.

DESERT HEADWEAR

French kepi
The space above the head creates an insulating pocket of air.

Tuareg veil The Saharan nomads favor blue cloth for sun and sand protection.

Cap and cloth
An effective improvised protection.

Safari hat
This African favorite has a wide brim and is permeable to air.

Dunes Desert dunes are created by windblown sand. The shape of a dune is influenced by the prevailing wind direction and the amount of sand available.

barchan

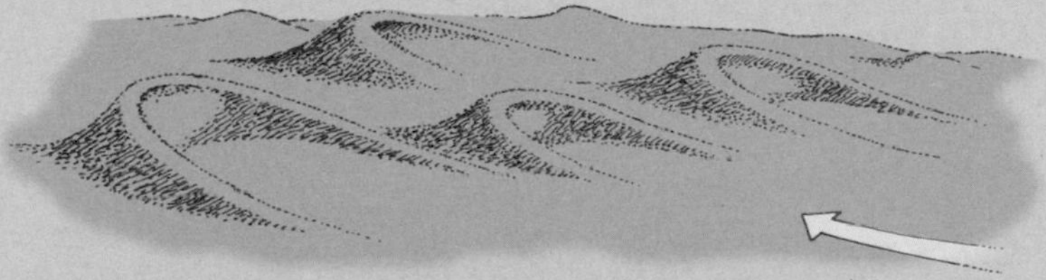

transverse

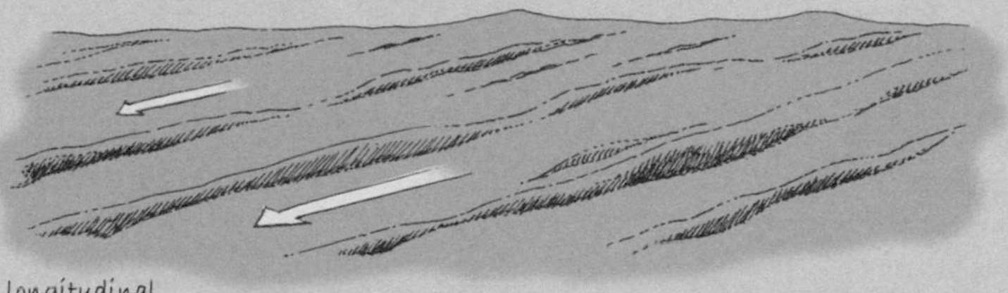

longitudinal

star

WINTER TRAVEL

Cold comforts Freezing conditions don't mean you have to stay indoors. With the right clothing and equipment, even the most frigid landscapes can be your winter wonderland.

OUTDOOR WINTER CLOTHING

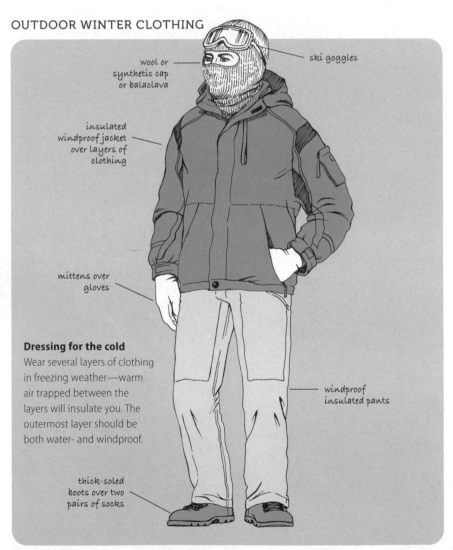

wool or synthetic cap or balaclava

ski goggles

insulated windproof jacket over layers of clothing

mittens over gloves

Dressing for the cold
Wear several layers of clothing in freezing weather—warm air trapped between the layers will insulate you. The outermost layer should be both water- and windproof.

windproof insulated pants

thick-soled boots over two pairs of socks

HEAT LOSS

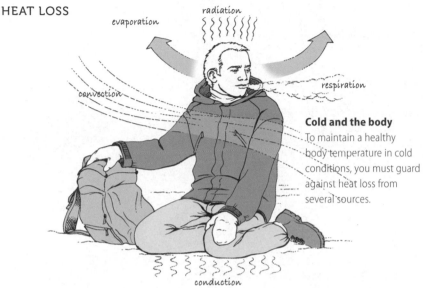

evaporation

radiation

respiration

convection

conduction

Cold and the body
To maintain a healthy body temperature in cold conditions, you must guard against heat loss from several sources.

Wet-weather fabrics
To stay warm, you must stay dry. The original waterproof fabric is oilskin—cotton impregnated with linseed oil. Polyurethane coated fabric is a cheaper and lighter synthetic alternative. Gore-Tex is a "breathable" fabric. It keeps water out while allowing perspiration to escape.

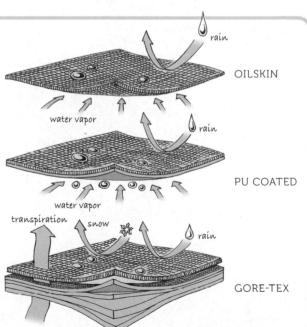

rain

OILSKIN

water vapor

rain

PU COATED

water vapor

transpiration

snow

rain

GORE-TEX

Cold weather gear In cold conditions, it's a good idea to pack a range of items that can be removed when exertion is greatest, and reapplied as needed, to stay warm when stopping to rest, or when the trail is easy.

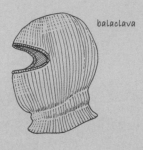
balaclava

synthetic beanie

woollen beanie

scarf

thermal underwear

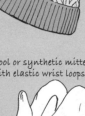
wool or synthetic mittens with elastic wrist loops

waterproof overmitts with elastic wrist loops

wool or thermal gloves

thermal vest

SNOWSHOES

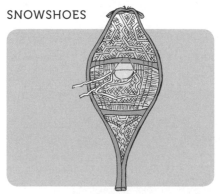

Attikamek traditional Snowshoes have been used in North America for thousands of years.

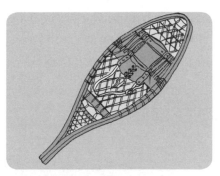

Mid-20th century Until recently, all snowshoes were made from timber and waxed rawhide.

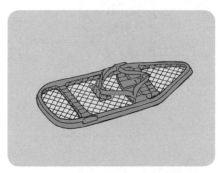

Canadian army These magnesium-framed snowshoes keep fully laden soldiers moving.

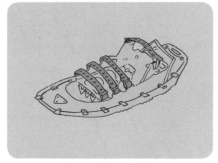

Modern civilian Modern snowshoes come in a wide variety of types to suit every need.

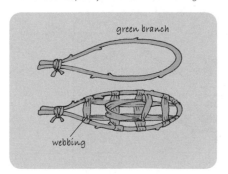

Improvised A green tree branch or sapling and webbing will make a serviceable snowshoe.

Emergency For a quick fix, an evergreen bough strapped to a shoe will work.

GLACIER HIKING

Walking on ice Glaciers are rivers of frozen ice found in the polar regions and many mountain ranges. It's always best to walk around them, unless you are part of an experienced team.

PARTS OF A GLACIER

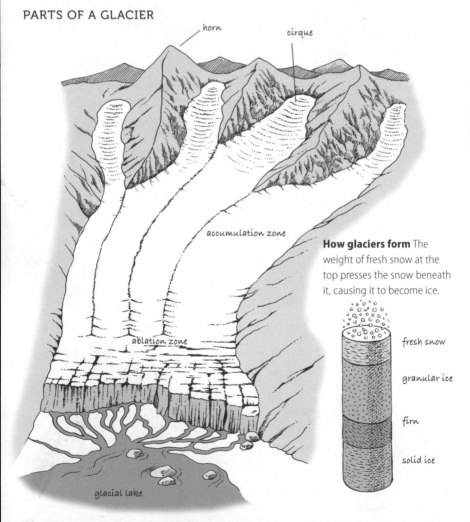

horn

cirque

accumulation zone

ablation zone

glacial lake

How glaciers form The weight of fresh snow at the top presses the snow beneath it, causing it to become ice.

fresh snow

granular ice

firn

solid ice

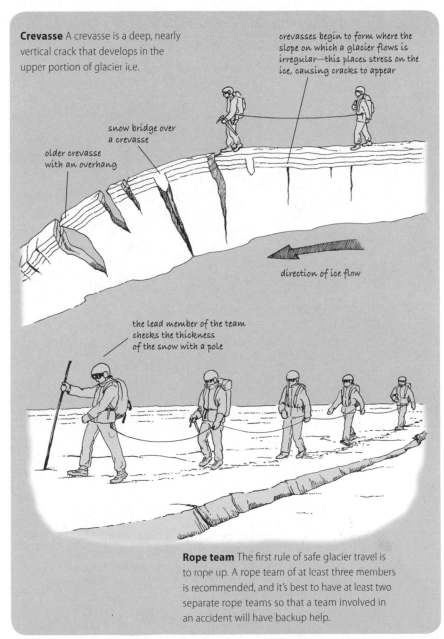

Crevasse A crevasse is a deep, nearly vertical crack that develops in the upper portion of glacier ice.

crevasses begin to form where the slope on which a glacier flows is irregular—this places stress on the ice, causing cracks to appear

snow bridge over a crevasse

older crevasse with an overhang

direction of ice flow

the lead member of the team checks the thickness of the snow with a pole

Rope team The first rule of safe glacier travel is to rope up. A rope team of at least three members is recommended, and it's best to have at least two separate rope teams so that a team involved in an accident will have backup help.

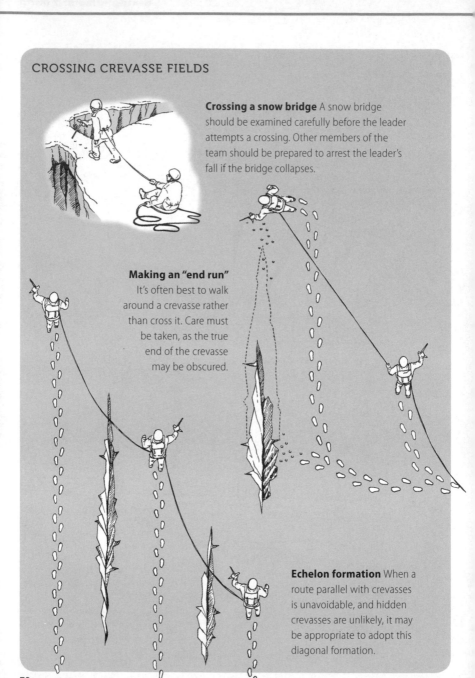

CROSSING CREVASSE FIELDS

Crossing a snow bridge A snow bridge should be examined carefully before the leader attempts a crossing. Other members of the team should be prepared to arrest the leader's fall if the bridge collapses.

Making an "end run" It's often best to walk around a crevasse rather than cross it. Care must be taken, as the true end of the crevasse may be obscured.

Echelon formation When a route parallel with crevasses is unavoidable, and hidden crevasses are unlikely, it may be appropriate to adopt this diagonal formation.

CREVASSE RESCUE KIT

Life saver This kit is an essential for glacier travel. It keeps everything required for a crevasse rescue in the one place.

1 When one member of a rope team falls into a crevasse, the other members of the team must immediately move into the self-arrest position (see page 185). This will stop the victim from falling any deeper into the crevasse.

2 If the fallen hiker is unable to ascend the rope, it is up to the other members of the rope team to effect a rescue. The rescuer closest to the victim releases self-arrest, and sets up a secure anchor in the snow. Refer to pages 195–8 for snow anchor options.

3 Once the anchor is secured, all members of the rope team outside the crevasse can work to haul the victim out. Unless the rope party is a large one, a pulley system will need to be set up.

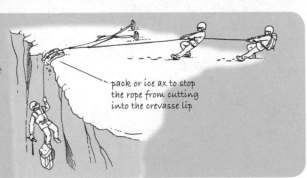

pack or ice ax to stop the rope from cutting into the crevasse lip

HILL WALKING

Grappling with gradients Hill walking is a great way to get fit, and many areas of great natural beauty happen to be hilly. Do it right and you'll have the stamina to cope with the ups and downs all day.

WALKING UPHILL

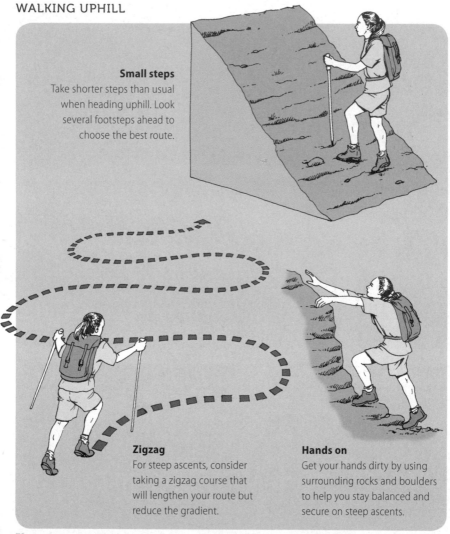

Small steps
Take shorter steps than usual when heading uphill. Look several footsteps ahead to choose the best route.

Zigzag
For steep ascents, consider taking a zigzag course that will lengthen your route but reduce the gradient.

Hands on
Get your hands dirty by using surrounding rocks and boulders to help you stay balanced and secure on steep ascents.

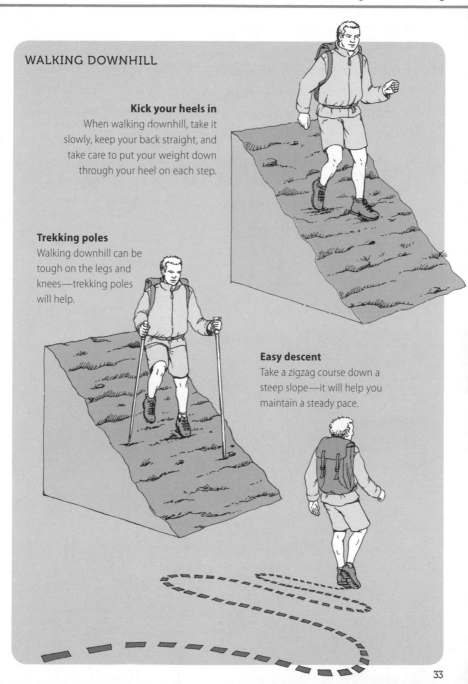

WALKING DOWNHILL

Kick your heels in
When walking downhill, take it slowly, keep your back straight, and take care to put your weight down through your heel on each step.

Trekking poles
Walking downhill can be tough on the legs and knees—trekking poles will help.

Easy descent
Take a zigzag course down a steep slope—it will help you maintain a steady pace.

CROSSING RIVERS

Many rivers to cross? A river without a bridge can be a formidable barrier. While there are many ways to get to the other side, remember that rivers and streams are always dangerous—approach them with care.

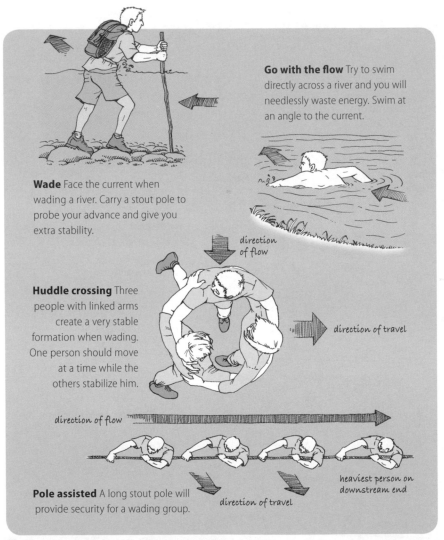

Go with the flow Try to swim directly across a river and you will needlessly waste energy. Swim at an angle to the current.

Wade Face the current when wading a river. Carry a stout pole to probe your advance and give you extra stability.

direction of flow

Huddle crossing Three people with linked arms create a very stable formation when wading. One person should move at a time while the others stabilize him.

direction of travel

direction of flow

Pole assisted A long stout pole will provide security for a wading group.

direction of travel

heaviest person on downstream end

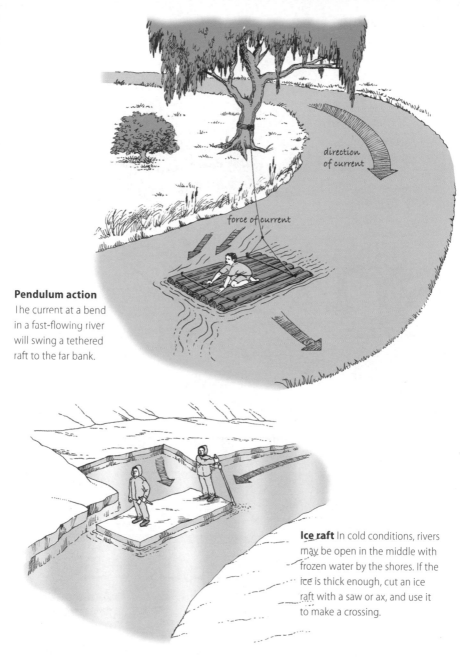

Pendulum action
The current at a bend in a fast-flowing river will swing a tethered raft to the far bank.

direction of current

force of current

Ice raft In cold conditions, rivers may be open in the middle with frozen water by the shores. If the ice is thick enough, cut an ice raft with a saw or ax, and use it to make a crossing.

ONE-ROPE BRIDGE

First across Check that the river is safe for the strongest member of the party to cross. The ideal site will have slow-flowing, shallow water. Once across, the swimmer/wader must securely anchor the end of the rope.

Pulled tight The remaining members of the party should make a slip knot on the rope and pull the rope taut.

FLOTATION AIDS

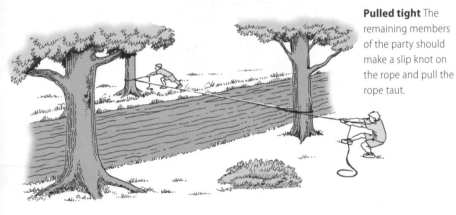

Water wings

1 Swing a pair of pants (with ankles tied) through the air at the surface.

2 Thrust the pants into the water, trapping air within.

3 You may have to refill the pants with air after a few minutes.

Rappel seat This is the preferred method. You will need a carabiner and a rappelling harness.

Monkey crawl Hang below the rope with hands and both heels crossed over the rope. Pull with your arms, and push your feet to make progress.

Commando crawl Lie on the rope with the right foot hooked on the rope. Let the left leg hang to maintain balance. Pull with your arms, and push your right foot to make progress.

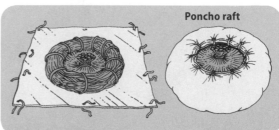

Poncho raft

Air mattress Keep your backpack loose so it can be ditched in a spill.

1 Tie the neck of the poncho and form a ring of plants around the center.

2 Gather up the extremities and tie in a ring around the top center.

MORE FLOTATION AIDS

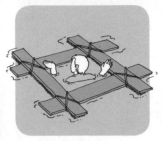

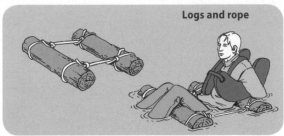

Logs and rope

Boards Four boards secured with rope or nails make a stable raft.

1 Find two short, dry logs, and tie them together with rope.

2 Seat yourself between the logs and start paddling with your hands.

MAKE A PONCHO EQUIPMENT RAFT

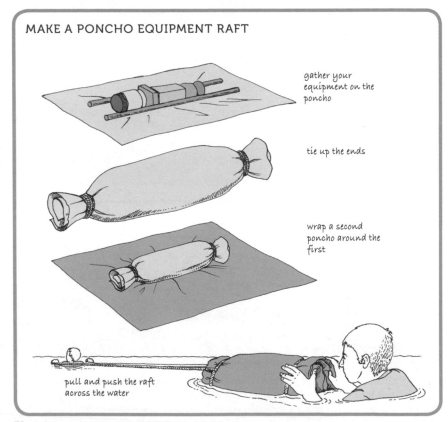

gather your equipment on the poncho

tie up the ends

wrap a second poncho around the first

pull and push the raft across the water

MAKE A RAFT

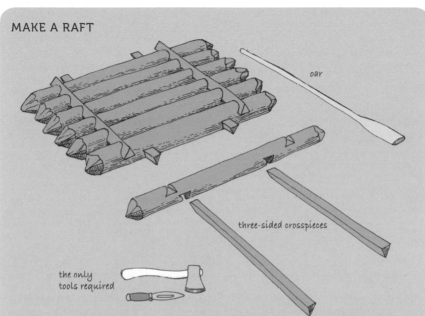

oar

three-sided crosspieces

the only tools required

River raft This raft for two or three people may take a day or two to build, but in rugged or jungle territory it may be the smartest way to get out of trouble.

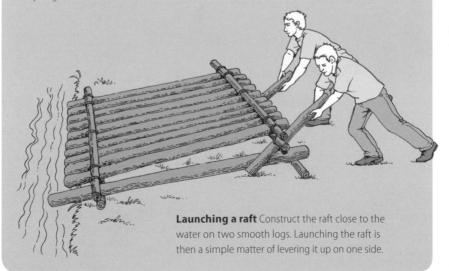

Launching a raft Construct the raft close to the water on two smooth logs. Launching the raft is then a simple matter of levering it up on one side.

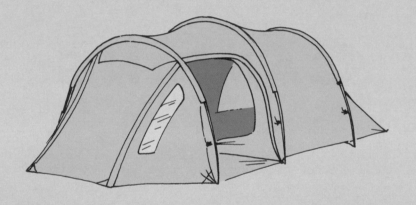

CAMPING

Whether you're under a tent, tarp, igloo, or the stars, a night outdoors can be either magical or miserable. Great camping is a matter of understanding your environment and packing the right gear.

CHOOSING A CAMPSITE

Location, location, location A good campsite will maximize your enjoyment of your surroundings, will have minimum impact on the environment, will allow you to relax, and will be safe.

THE IDEAL CAMPSITE

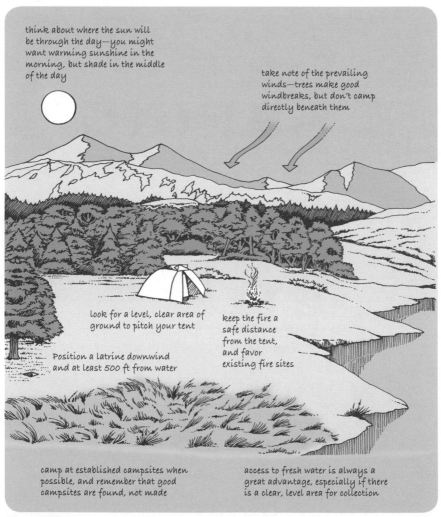

think about where the sun will be through the day—you might want warming sunshine in the morning, but shade in the middle of the day

take note of the prevailing winds—trees make good windbreaks, but don't camp directly beneath them

look for a level, clear area of ground to pitch your tent

keep the fire a safe distance from the tent, and favor existing fire sites

Position a latrine downwind and at least 500 ft from water

camp at established campsites when possible, and remember that good campsites are found, not made

access to fresh water is always a great advantage, especially if there is a clear, level area for collection

WHERE NOT TO CAMP

Flood risk Washouts, gullies, and floodplains can be deadly when it rains. Even distant rainfall can mean danger downstream.

Under a tree Even healthy-looking branches may drop without warning. Look up—if there are heavy limbs above, move elsewhere.

Cliff base Don't camp below a cliff or steep rocky slope, especially if the area is littered with freshly broken stones.

Avalanche risk Stay away from steep slopes during or after heavy snowfall—an avalanche may follow without warning.

TENTS

Home away from home A good tent is your haven from wind, rain, cold temperatures, and blazing sun. Choose well and your tent will be your best friend.

A-frame

dome with fly

dome without fly

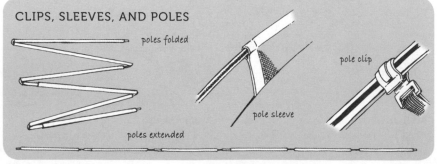

CLIPS, SLEEVES, AND POLES

poles folded

pole clip

pole sleeve

poles extended

OTHER TENT TYPES

geodesic

three-hoop

two-hoop

family

self-erecting

45

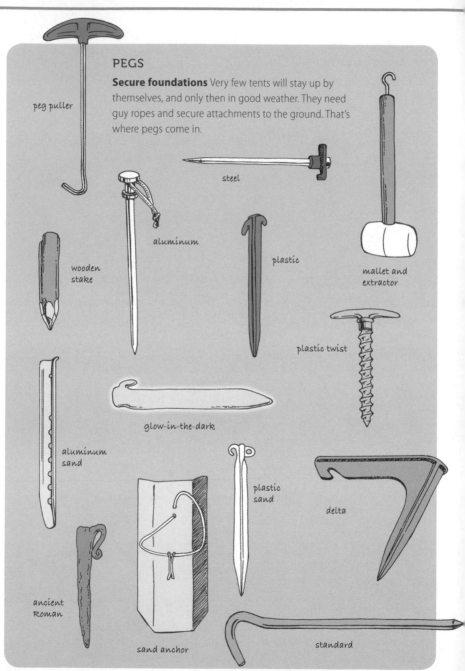

PEGS

Secure foundations Very few tents will stay up by themselves, and only then in good weather. They need guy ropes and secure attachments to the ground. That's where pegs come in.

peg puller

steel

aluminum

plastic

mallet and extractor

wooden stake

plastic twist

glow-in-the-dark

aluminum sand

plastic sand

delta

ancient Roman

sand anchor

standard

PLACING PEGS

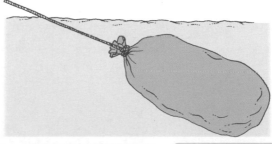

Mountain favorite
A buried sleeping bag stuff sack filled with snow makes a secure alpine anchor.

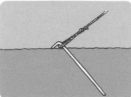

Standard This is the correct way to secure a peg—the rope is at 90 degrees to the peg.

Super stable When stability is vital, secure the head of your first peg with another.

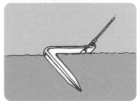

Delta These pegs keep leverage at a minimum for a very secure hold.

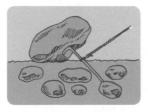

Backup Use a heavy rock to secure a peg when it can't go deep into rocky ground.

Rocks Turn an excess of rocks to your advantage by using them to anchor your lines.

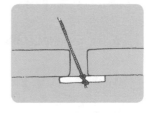

Ice For a frozen fastener, tie your tent line to a peg passed through a hole in the ice.

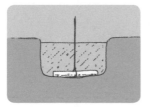

Sand A peg or small log buried deep in sand makes a good desert anchor.

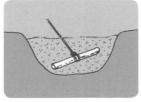

Ice Place a peg in a hole in the snow. Then, fill with water. Soon you'll have an anchor in ice.

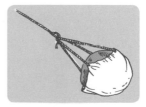

Parachute Scoop sand, snow, or rocks into a parachute anchor, then bury it.

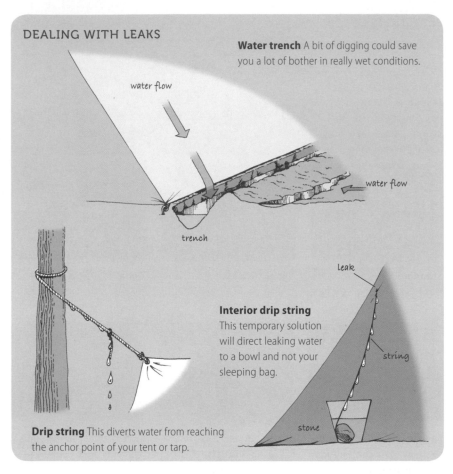

DEALING WITH LEAKS

Water trench A bit of digging could save you a lot of bother in really wet conditions.

water flow

water flow

trench

Interior drip string This temporary solution will direct leaking water to a bowl and not your sleeping bag.

leak

string

stone

Drip string This diverts water from reaching the anchor point of your tent or tarp.

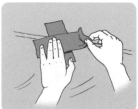

Quick fix Apply duct tape to a hole or split seam. This is best done when it isn't raining.

Hole patch Cheap adhesive patch kits will permanently seal a leaking hole.

Seam sealer Leaks often occur along seams. Fix them with adhesive seam sealer.

OTHER SHELTERS

Tarps, tepees, and more A tent isn't the only option for shelter in the outdoors, in fact in many conditions, you'd be better off with something quite different.

The art of tarp Tarpaulins are simple rectangles of waterproof fabric, often with anchor points at each corner. They make versatile lightweight shelters.

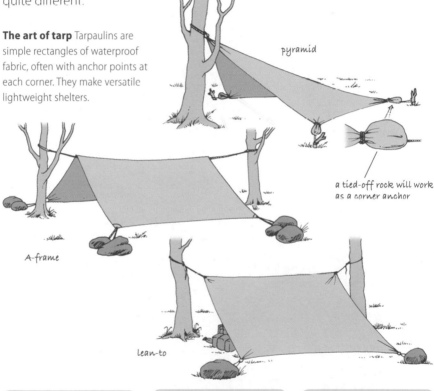

pyramid

a tied-off rock will work as a corner anchor

A-frame

lean-to

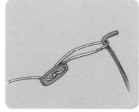

Plastic line tensioner These devices will tighten guy lines with a simple tugging motion.

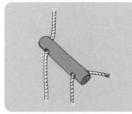

Timber line tensioner For guy ropes, a piece of timber with two holes will do the job.

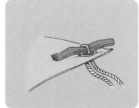

Stick anchor This arrangement will save wear on your tarpaulin corner grommets.

MORE SHELTERS

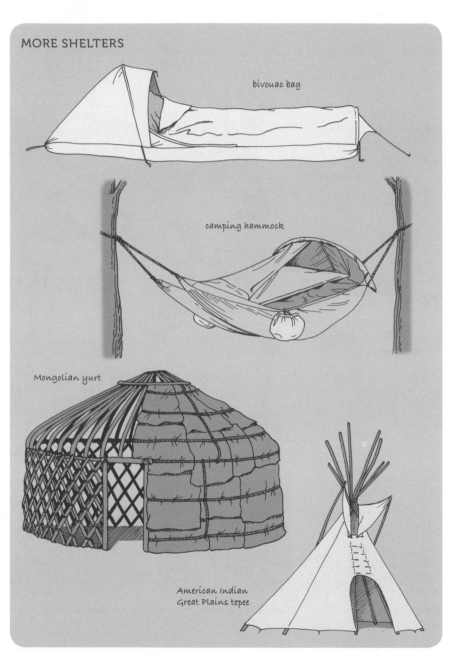

bivouac bag

camping hammock

Mongolian yurt

American Indian
Great Plains tepee

SNOW AND ICE SHELTERS

Snow cave With experience and a snow shovel, you and a friend can build a comfortable snow cave in a couple of hours. They can be a life-saver, but be alert to the risks of carbon monoxide poisoning.

ventilation hole—essential!

skis or other equipment to alert your position to others

Igloo This Inuit invention remains an option for shelter in cold conditions.

HOW TO MAKE AN IGLOO

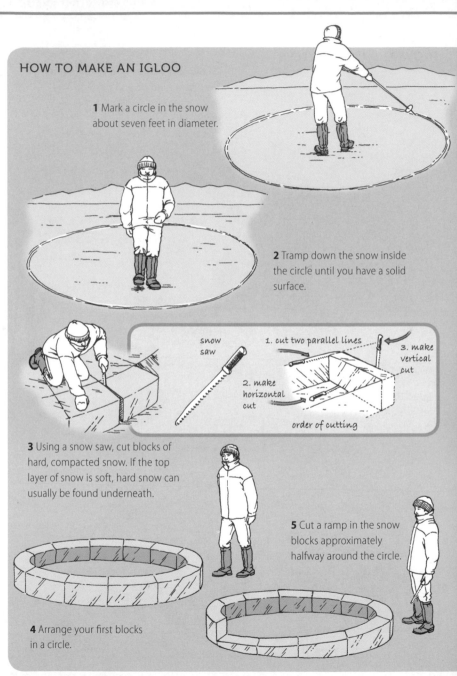

1 Mark a circle in the snow about seven feet in diameter.

2 Tramp down the snow inside the circle until you have a solid surface.

snow saw

1. cut two parallel lines

2. make horizontal cut

3. make vertical cut

order of cutting

3 Using a snow saw, cut blocks of hard, compacted snow. If the top layer of snow is soft, hard snow can usually be found underneath.

5 Cut a ramp in the snow blocks approximately halfway around the circle.

4 Arrange your first blocks in a circle.

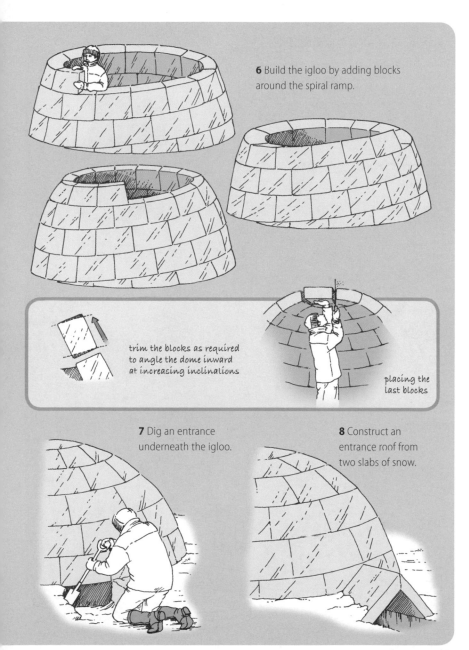

6 Build the igloo by adding blocks around the spiral ramp.

trim the blocks as required to angle the dome inward at increasing inclinations

placing the last blocks

7 Dig an entrance underneath the igloo.

8 Construct an entrance roof from two slabs of snow.

HOW TO MAKE A QUINZEE

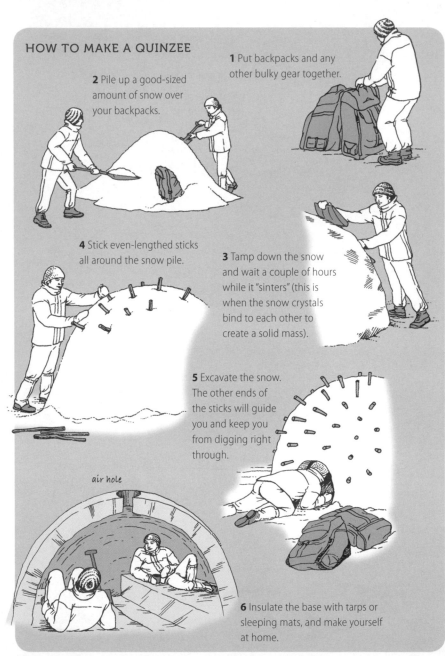

1 Put backpacks and any other bulky gear together.

2 Pile up a good-sized amount of snow over your backpacks.

3 Tamp down the snow and wait a couple of hours while it "sinters" (this is when the snow crystals bind to each other to create a solid mass).

4 Stick even-lengthed sticks all around the snow pile.

5 Excavate the snow. The other ends of the sticks will guide you and keep you from digging right through.

air hole

6 Insulate the base with tarps or sleeping mats, and make yourself at home.

SLEEPING BAGS

Get snug A good-quality sleeping bag appropriate to the season is essential for a good night's sleep and a happy experience in the outdoors. If you hike or camp year-round, you might need more than one.

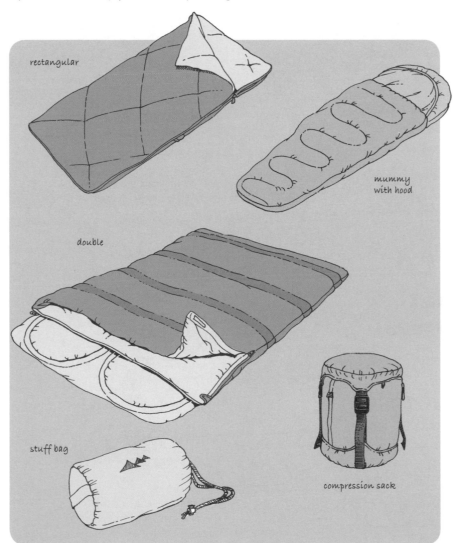

rectangular

mummy with hood

double

stuff bag

compression sack

SLEEPING BAG CONSTRUCTION

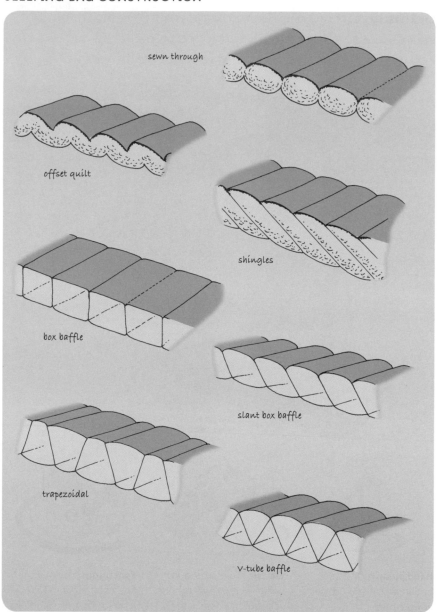

sewn through

offset quilt

shingles

box baffle

slant box baffle

trapezoidal

v-tube baffle

SLEEPING SOFTLY

On the level A camping mattress provides both comfort and thermal insulation from cold ground.

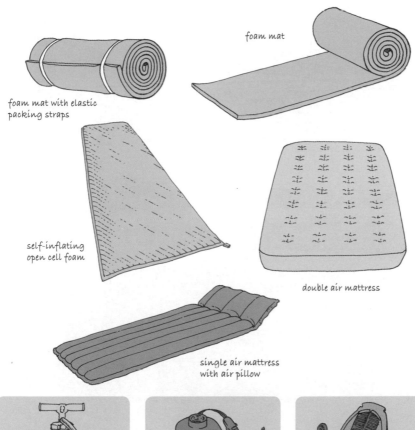

foam mat

foam mat with elastic packing straps

self-inflating open cell foam

double air mattress

single air mattress with air pillow

Hand pump Hand pumps operate on both the up and down strokes.

Electric These labor-saving pumps work off a vehicle's 12 volt auxiliary power outlet.

Foot pump Keep your hands free for other things with reinforced nylon foot bellows.

KNIVES

The crucial tool A good sharp knife is a camping essential. They are available as either fixed blades or folding blades. The latter often come with a host of other useful tools.

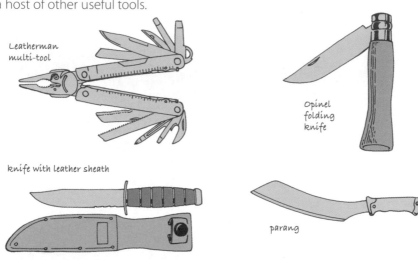

Leatherman multi-tool

Opinel folding knife

knife with leather sheath

parang

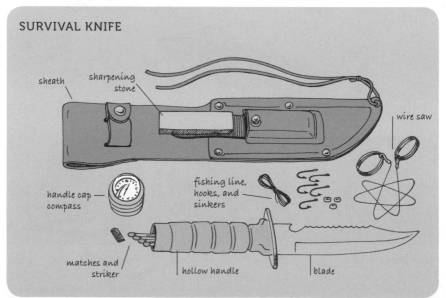

SURVIVAL KNIFE

sheath

sharpening stone

wire saw

handle cap compass

fishing line, hooks, and sinkers

matches and striker

hollow handle

blade

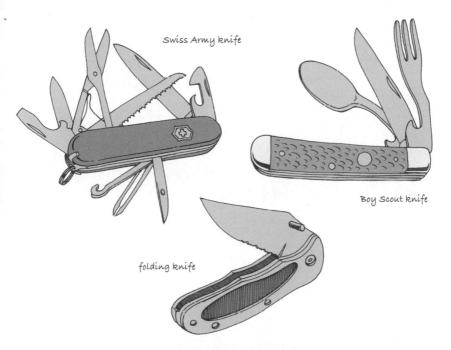

Swiss Army knife

Boy Scout knife

folding knife

ANATOMY OF A HUNTING KNIFE

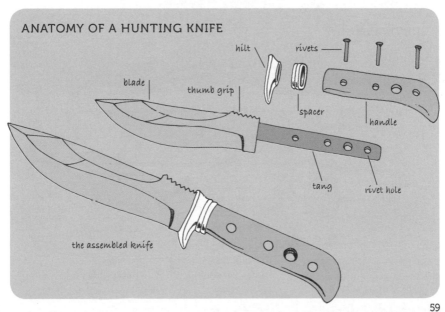

hilt

rivets

blade

thumb grip

spacer

handle

tang

rivet hole

the assembled knife

KNIVES THROUGH HISTORY

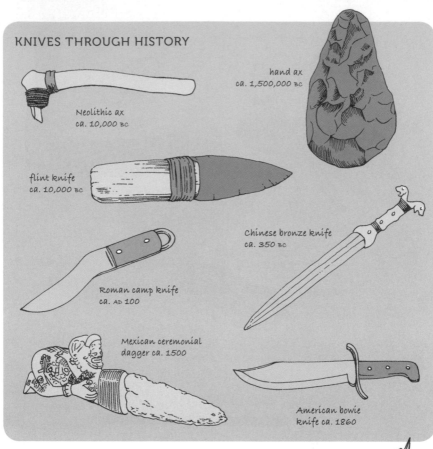

hand ax
ca. 1,500,000 BC

Neolithic ax
ca. 10,000 BC

flint knife
ca. 10,000 BC

Chinese bronze knife
ca. 350 BC

Roman camp knife
ca. AD 100

Mexican ceremonial
dagger ca. 1500

American bowie
knife ca. 1860

Chop Use only large blades for chopping. Bring the main part of the blade across the grain of the wood at 45 degrees.

Whittle This type of fine carving is best done with a small knife. Use your thumb to guide the blade.

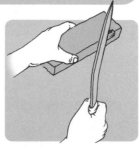

Carve Always keep fingers and limbs out of the way when carving. Make shallow cuts along the grain of the wood.

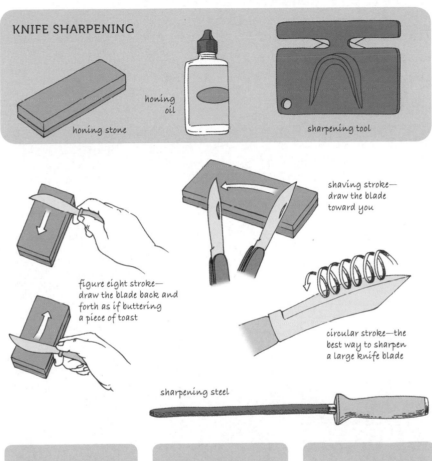

KNIFE SHARPENING

honing stone

honing oil

sharpening tool

shaving stroke—draw the blade toward you

figure eight stroke—draw the blade back and forth as if buttering a piece of toast

circular stroke—the best way to sharpen a large knife blade

sharpening steel

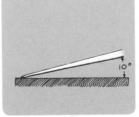

10 degrees For light duty and fine work such as filleting and shaving. The edge will blunt fairly quickly.

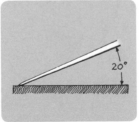

20 degrees A good angle for everyday use. To approximate it, imagine half of 90 degrees, then half of 45 degrees.

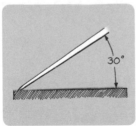

30 degrees A somewhat blunt yet long-lasting edge for heavy-duty work, such as chopping wood.

TOILET AND SHOWER

The bathroom outdoors The call of nature doesn't take a break when you're surrounded by nature. For a healthy environment and a healthy you, it's essential to maintain hygiene when outdoors.

THE LATRINE

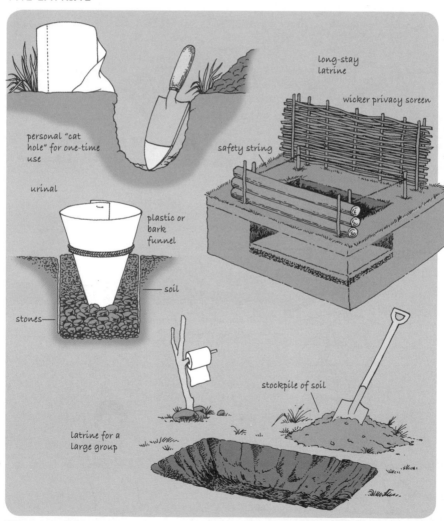

personal "cat hole" for one-time use

long-stay latrine

wicker privacy screen

safety string

urinal

plastic or bark funnel

soil

stones

latrine for a large group

stockpile of soil

KEEPING CLEAN

hand wash

antibacterial wipes

soap

USING A SOLAR SHOWER

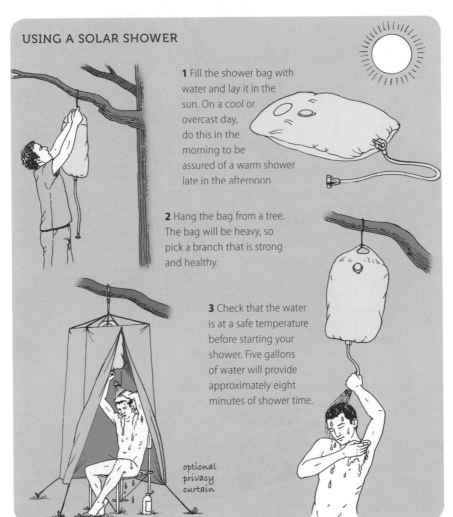

1 Fill the shower bag with water and lay it in the sun. On a cool or overcast day, do this in the morning to be assured of a warm shower late in the afternoon.

2 Hang the bag from a tree. The bag will be heavy, so pick a branch that is strong and healthy.

3 Check that the water is at a safe temperature before starting your shower. Five gallons of water will provide approximately eight minutes of shower time.

optional privacy curtain

Food caches

Don't feed the animals You don't want to share your precious supplies with the local wildlife. You might go hungry and it's bad for their welfare. Hungry bears present a particular challenge.

BEAR CACHES

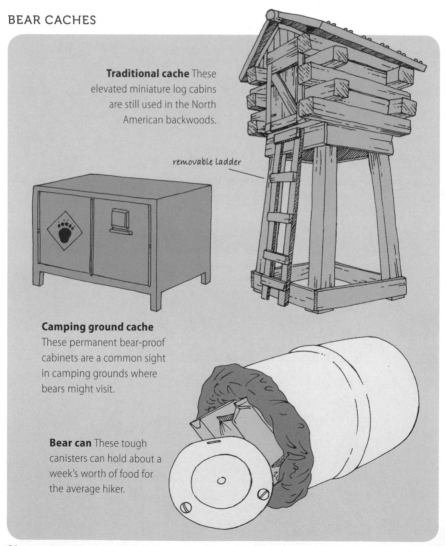

Traditional cache These elevated miniature log cabins are still used in the North American backwoods.

removable ladder

Camping ground cache These permanent bear-proof cabinets are a common sight in camping grounds where bears might visit.

Bear can These tough canisters can hold about a week's worth of food for the average hiker.

SETTING UP A THROWLINE BEAR CACHE

1 Find two trees located about 15 feet apart. Throw the line over a branch about 15 feet up.

2 Tie the line to the trunk of the first tree then throw the line over a branch of the second tree.

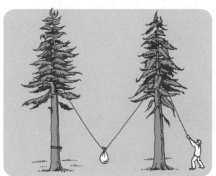

3 Secure your food bag to the line. Then, hoist it up until it's at least 12 feet above the ground.

4 Tie the other end of the line to the trunk of the second tree. Your food is now secured.

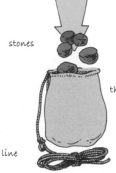

stones

throw bag

line

Throw bag To prime the throw bag, fill it with rocks and tighten the drawstring.

COOKING

Some of the best meals you will ever taste will
be those you have prepared over a campfire or
camping stove, and consumed under the stars.

Nutrition

Eating well Good nutrition is the key to good health. This is especially true if you are getting active outdoors. An active body requires a balanced intake of water, various food groups, vitamins, and minerals.

WATER

The stuff of life The most vital substance in our bodies is water. It makes up more than half of the body by weight, and fulfills such crucial roles that a few days without it can amount to a death sentence.

MICRONUTRIENTS

Essential elements Micronutrients are essential vitamins and minerals that are needed in very small quantities for various physiological functions. Examples include salt and the vitamins and minerals found in leafy vegetables, fruit, and vitamin supplements.

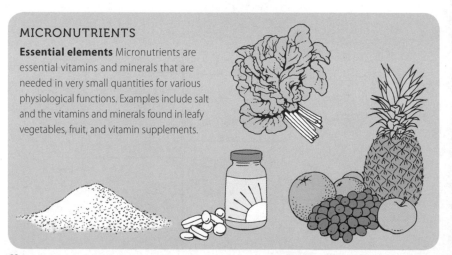

CARBOHYDRATES

Energy foods Carbohydrates are the body's prime energy source. They are found in abundance in bread, pasta, rice, potatoes, fruit, and sweets.

FATS

Greasy goodness Fats are essential for processing some vitamins, promoting healthy cell function, and are a rich source of energy.

PROTEIN

Body builder Protein builds up, maintains, and replaces the tissues in your body. It is essential for muscle growth and a healthy immune system.

MYPLATE

Guide to healthy eating

MyPlate is a graphic guide to a healthy meal. Half your plate should be fruits and vegetables. Cut down on big portion sizes, extra fats, and foods that are high in sugar and sodium.

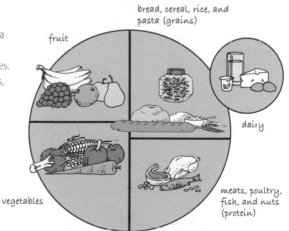

fruit

bread, cereal, rice, and pasta (grains)

dairy

vegetables

meats, poultry, fish, and nuts (protein)

FOOD FOR THE OUTDOORS

A larder on your back Just as it is at home, a healthy diet is essential when you are enjoying the outdoors. Plan carefully for food that is healthy, tasty, lightweight, and doesn't need refrigeration.

FOOD ON THE MOVE

Hiking fuel If you're on a big hike, your body will need a lot more food than normal. Graze on these easily digested, energy-rich foods and you can keep going for hours.

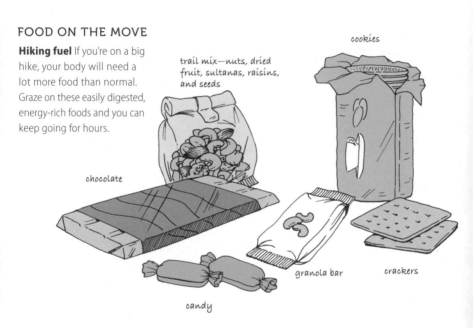

cookies

trail mix—nuts, dried fruit, sultanas, raisins, and seeds

chocolate

granola bar

crackers

candy

BREAKFAST

long-life milk

powdered milk

oatmeal

cereal

tea & coffee

fruit

eggs in egg case

bacon

bagels

flatbread

A good start A good breakfast will set you up for the rest of the day. Breakfast cereals, along with fruit and bread, is a healthy combination. Bacon and eggs are great if it's going to be an active day.

Midday meal It's usually easiest to save the cooking for the evening. Make a sandwich or a salad for lunch, supplemented with fruit, cheese, canned fish, or salami.

Night feast Construct your evening meal around a carbohydrate-rich base of pasta, rice, or potatoes, with supplemental protein from meat, lentils, or beans.

Treat yourself A sweet treat in the wilderness is one of life's true luxuries. And if you've been moving all day, you don't have to worry about the calories!

FIRE MAKING

Foundations for flame Humans have been making cooking and campfires for a few hundred thousand years now. But is this a skill that's lost on you? If so, read on.

FIRE TRIANGLE

Recipe for combustion There are three elements that must be present for a fire to exist: oxygen, fuel, and heat. You'll need them in the right combination to get your fire started. Conversely, removing one or more of these elements is the key to extinguishing a fire that has started.

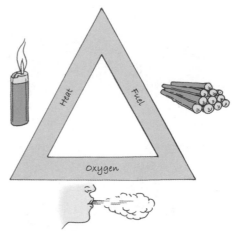

TINDER

Bark Look for dry inner bark from dead logs.

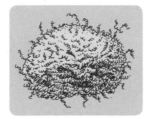

Moss Dead, dry moss makes an excellent fire starter.

Grass Break down stalks of dry grass into fine fibers.

Fungus The inner flesh from bracket fungus is flammable.

Cotton balls and petroleum jelly A highly flammable mix.

Leaves Dry dead leaves can always be found if you look.

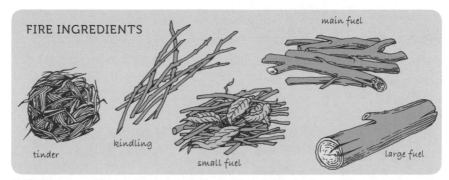

FIRE INGREDIENTS

main fuel

tinder

kindling

small fuel

large fuel

Build it up A good fire is built up gradually. Start with tinder—a fine flammable material that easily catches a spark. Once the tinder has begun to burn, add kindling—dry twigs and sticks no thicker than your little finger. As coals are created, progressively add larger pieces of fuel.

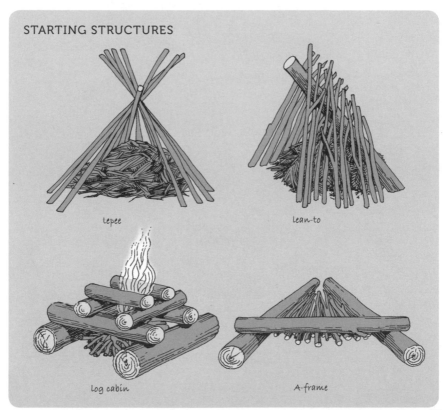

STARTING STRUCTURES

tepee

lean-to

log cabin

A-frame

FIRE STARTING

We have ignition Starting fires has been a pretty straightforward task since the invention of matches (and then lighters). But could you get things blazing without these tools?

HEAT SOURCE

lighter

matches

magnifying glass

ice sphere

rotate the sphere
until a good focus
point is found

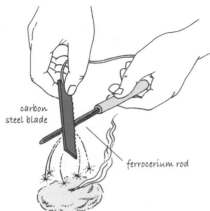

Parabolic can Polish the base of a soda can with chocolate or toothpaste until it is mirror smooth (this may take several hours). Focused sunlight will ignite tinder.

Flint and steel The "flint" component of a flint and steel fire-starting kit is actually made of a metal alloy called ferrocerium. When struck with steel, it emits a shower of sparks.

BATTERY METHOD

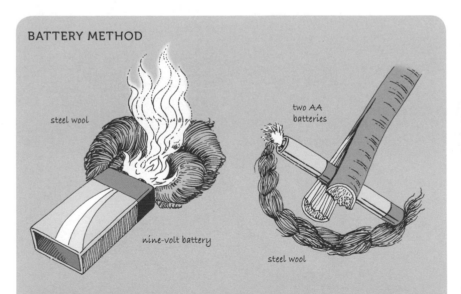

Electric spark When steel wool is brushed against the contacts of a battery, it will glow brightly and begin to burn. A nine-volt battery is most convenient for this method, but any battery will work, including one from a cell phone.

MAGNESIUM FIRE BLOCK

Chip off the block These fire-starting kits consist of a steel striker and a block of magnesium with a ferrocerium rod fixed down one side. They are small, light, and are still effective in damp conditions.

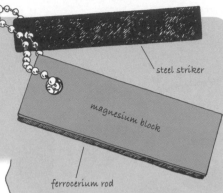

steel striker

magnesium block

ferrocerium rod

1 To begin, use a knife blade to scrape a small pile of shavings from the magnesium block. The shavings are light, so protect the pile from the breeze.

2 Collect the shavings and gather them in a little nest of dry tinder.

3 Run the ferrocerium rod along the steel striker or a knife blade. The resulting sparks will catch in the magnesium shavings and burn a very intense, white-hot flame for a few seconds—long enough to get your kindling burning.

HAND DRILL

Fire by hand A hand drill consists of a softwood drill and fireboard. Run your hands down the drill as you spin it, to maintain pressure and build friction.

drill

fireboard

tinder

FIRE PISTON

Squeeze and spark This ancient device from Southeast Asia and the Pacific uses the heat generated by the rapid compression of air to ignite tinder held at the end of the piston.

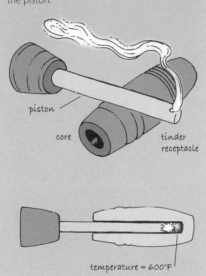

piston

core

tinder receptacle

temperature ≈ 600°F

FIRE PLOUGH

Get into the groove Cut a straight groove along a softwood base. Plough the tip of a hardwood rod back and forth along this groove. As friction builds up, small wood fibers will become detached from the groove. Eventually the detached fibers will start smoldering and form a "coal." Use this to ignite your tinder.

smoldering fibers

BOW DRILL

Drill for fire The bow drill is slightly more complicated than other friction fire-starting methods, but once mastered, it is extremely effective—even in circumstances when cool temperatures and humidity are working against you.

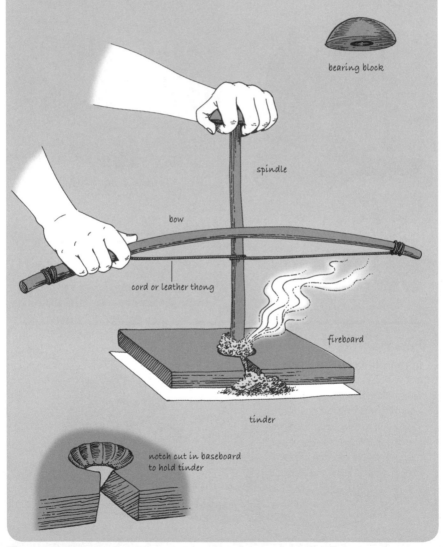

bearing block

spindle

bow

cord or leather thong

fireboard

tinder

notch cut in baseboard to hold tinder

BLOWING TINDER

Coaxing a flame The end result of many fire-starting methods is not flame but a precious glowing ember. To really get the fire started, quickly gather the ember into a bundle of tinder and blow gently. This adds oxygen and raises the temperature sufficiently to cause combustion.

CARRYING FIRE

Keeper of the flame It can be easier to carry embers rather than to start a fire without matches or a lighter. To do this, punch a few holes in a can and attach a string or wire for a handle. Then sandwich the embers between two layers of dry moss. Check the embers from time to time, and blow on them if they are losing potency. Well cared for, the embers should last several days.

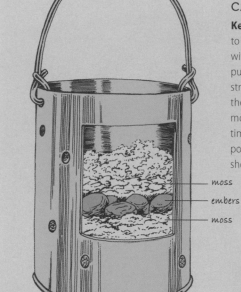

moss
embers
moss

COOKING WITH FIRE

Security, socializing, and sustenance Apart from offering a centerpiece for warmth and friendship, the main purpose of campfires is to cook your own food.

CAMPFIRE OPTIONS

Stable fireplace Use three stones to support the pot.

Natural skewers Fish and meat can be grilled on sticks over the fire.

Handy branches Using a support branch to control height, a forked branch can hold several utensils.

Wind assisted The open side of a three-sided fireplace should face into the wind.

Basic construction Put two logs parallel to the wind to form a simple fireplace.

An easy spit Sharpened branches driven into the ground offer a sturdy spit at the right height.

Uneven surface Use the slope of the ground to help support your utensils over the fire.

Longer term If you are staying in one place for a while, dig a hole for a more permanent fireplace.

Star fire Push in the logs as they burn to create a long-lasting cooking spot.

Crane This arrangement will keep your cooking pot off the fire, and keep it from getting smothered.

Adjustable crane The adjustable crane gives you the temperature control you thought you had left back in the kitchen at home.

Stone griddle A slab of stone will take a long time to heat, but will stay hot for a long time. Don't use a slab of porous or damp stone—it might explode.

Bamboo cooking pot
Green bamboo is very fire resistant and makes an excellent pot for boiling and simmering.

food goes here

steam

water

Bamboo steamer Punch a few holes in each of the two walls that divide a length of bamboo into three sections. Put water in one end and food in the other and you have a steamer.

Foil oven Wrap a whole meal in aluminum foil and put it into the coals for a slow roast. By using this method exclusively, you can save on the weight of cooking pots and pans.

Breakfast in a bag Line the bottom of a damp paper bag with bacon, then crack an egg on top. Place the bag on some hot coals and ashes to cook.

HANGI

Buried feast The hangi is a traditional New Zealand Maori method of cooking large communal meals. To make a hangi, first dig a pit in the ground. Then build a pyre of wood beams over the pit to carry the hangi stones. Set the pyre ablaze to super-heat the stones. Once they have dropped into the pit, add the food in wire baskets, cover in damp sacks and soil, and leave to cook for two to three hours.

soil

damp burlap sacks

hot rocks

MUD BAKING

1 Gut a fish or bird and lay it on a bed of non-poisonous green leaves. There is no need to remove the scales or feathers.

2 Fold the leaves over the fish or bird, ensuring that it is completely covered. Bind the package with twine.

3 Pack mud all around the package. Use clay if it is available, or use mud that has a clay texture. Check that there are no holes.

4 Bury the package in hot coals. A medium-sized fish or bird should take about 20 minutes to cook.

CAMPING STOVES

Cooking clean Preparing meals on an open fire has its downsides. Things get sooty, and collecting fuel means taking a resource from nature. Often, a camping stove is the right way to get cooking outdoors.

FUEL STOVES

multi-fuel stove

butane/propane cartridge
and burner attachment

double burner

single burner with
butane canister

ALCOHOL BURNER SET

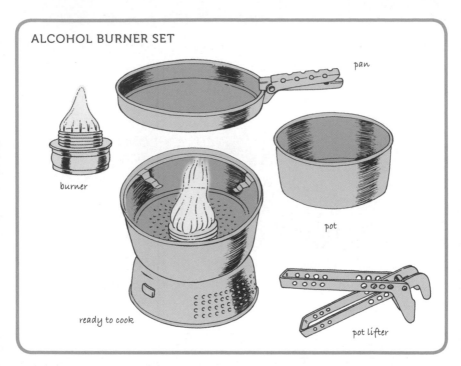

burner

pan

pot

ready to cook

pot lifter

Primus paraffin stove Invented in 1892, the Primus pressurized paraffin burner was the original camping and expedition stove.

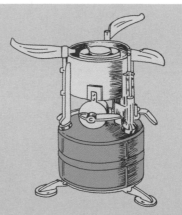

US Army gasoline-burning stove These stoves were standard US Army issue from 1951 until 1987.

COOKING WITHOUT GAS

Parabolic solar cooker

Solar cookers are the ultimate in environmentally friendly cooking. Parabolic cookers can reach high temperatures very quickly and are good for bringing liquids to a boil.

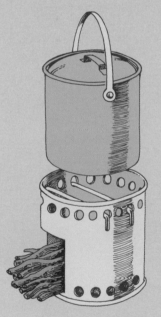

Twig stove This low-impact twig burner can be easily constructed from a steel can and wire using basic tools.

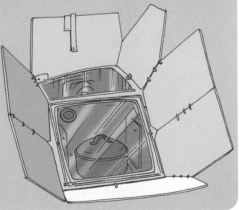

Solar box oven This design incorporates reflective panels and a sealed light-absorbent chamber. Temperatures inside can typically reach 300°F.

Cooking Utensils

Tools for cooking, serving, and washing You don't need to bring everything but the kitchen sink to be properly equipped for outdoor cooking and dining. Choose carefully, pack light, and you'll be all right.

THE CAMP COOKING ESSENTIALS

nesting pot set

mess tins

tin can pot

cast iron skillet

spoon and spatula

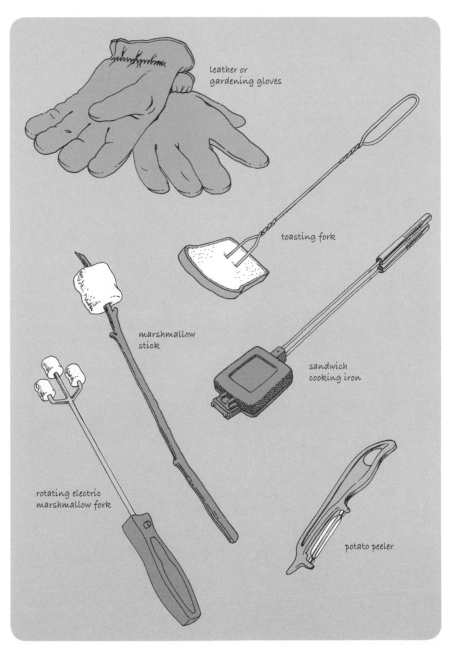

leather or gardening gloves

toasting fork

marshmallow stick

sandwich cooking iron

rotating electric marshmallow fork

potato peeler

plate

bowl

mug

camping
cutlery set

spork

collapsible cup

coffee pot

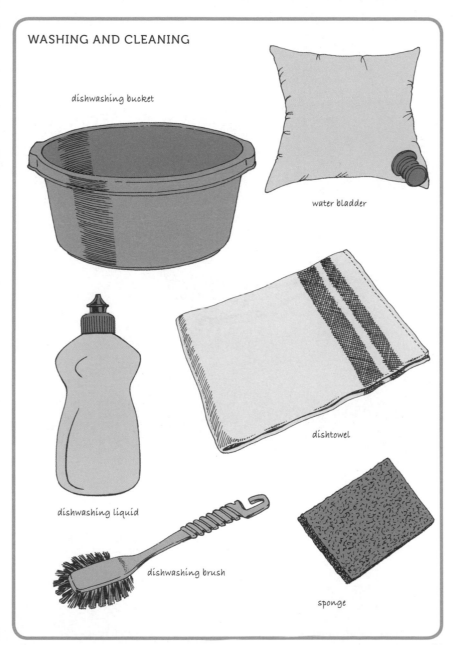

WASHING AND CLEANING

dishwashing bucket

water bladder

dishwashing liquid

dishtowel

dishwashing brush

sponge

FISHING

Fishing is one of the most popular recreational activities worldwide. From a hook and a hand line to big game ocean fishing, it offers something for everyone who enjoys a relaxing day outdoors.

ROD AND REEL

Line management You can catch a fish with nothing more than a line and hook, but add a rod and a reel to your armory, and you'll be able to cast further and exercise more control over a hooked fish.

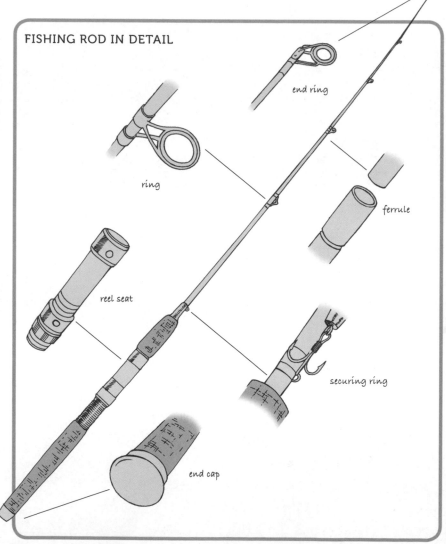

FISHING ROD IN DETAIL

end ring

ring

ferrule

reel seat

securing ring

end cap

FLY REEL

Reel simple The reel is far less important for fly-fishing than it is with bait or sea fishing. The reel's primary purpose when fly-fishing is to hold neatly the line that you are not using. Most fly reels are of simple single action design— meaning each complete turn of the handle equals one complete turn of the spool. If you are casting for powerful fish, such as salmon, pick a good quality fly reel with a smooth one-way drag system.

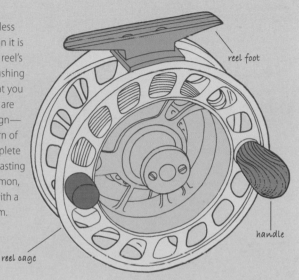

reel foot

handle

reel cage

FIXED-SPOOL REEL

The all-arounder As the name suggests, these reels have spools that don't rotate when the line is being retrieved. Instead, the line is wrapped around the spool by a bail rotor, carrying a bail arm and bail roller. When casting, the rotating bail is lifted which allows the line to run off the spool. Also known as threadline, or spinning reels, these are the reel of choice for most anglers for most situations.

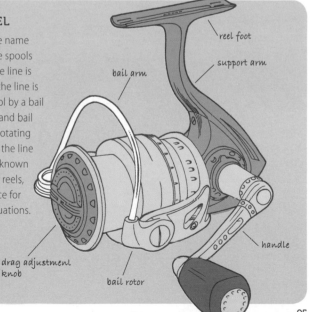

reel foot

support arm

bail arm

drag adjustment knob

bail rotor

handle

BAITCASTING REEL

Overhead revolver
The main characteristic of a baitcasting reel is that it is mounted above the fishing rod, where the line is stored on a revolving spool. With a bit of practice, a baitcasting reel can allow you to make long casts with terrific accuracy.

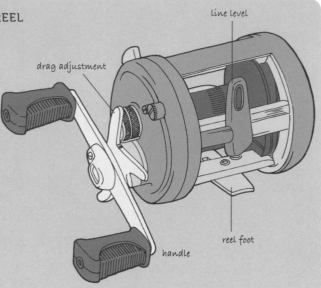

line level

drag adjustment

reel foot

handle

SPINCAST REEL

Press a button Also called closed-face reels, spincast reels are simple to operate and often inexpensive. To use a spincast reel, press the button on the back of the reel during your forward cast. The line runs out until you let go of the button that stops the line.

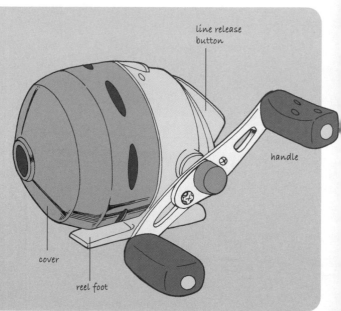

line release button

handle

cover

reel foot

ATTACH A REEL

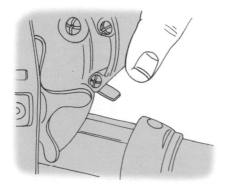 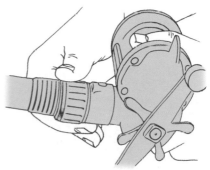

1 Turn the rod over so the reel seat is facing up. Slip one end of the reel foot underneath the non-moving hood of the reel seat.

2 Slide the other reel seat over the other end of the reel foot, and tighten the retainer ring until the reel is firmly attached.

LOAD AN OVERHEAD REEL

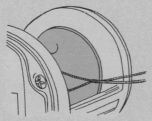 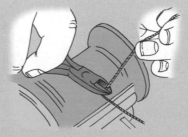

2 Trim the excess line with snips, and you are ready to start filling the reel.

1 Attach your reel to your rod before you begin. Feed the line through the line level, if present. Then, tie the line directly to the center of the spool, using a secure knot.

3 Have an assistant hold the filler spool. Begin reeling the line in. Use your thumb to spread the line across the spool smoothly and evenly.

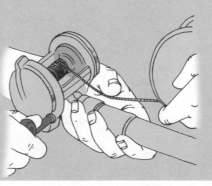

LOAD A FIXED-SPOOL REEL

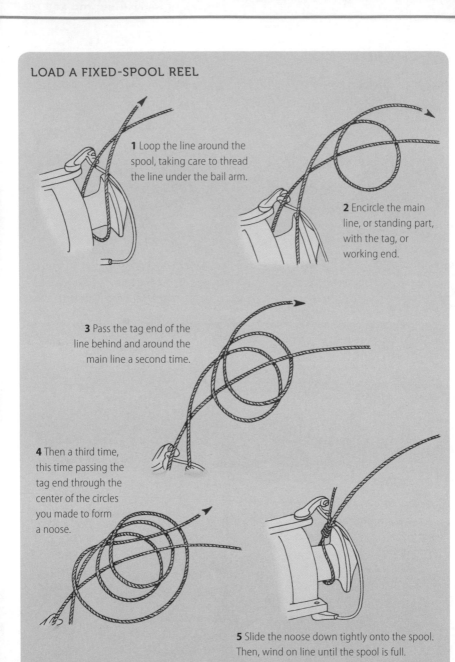

1 Loop the line around the spool, taking care to thread the line under the bail arm.

2 Encircle the main line, or standing part, with the tag, or working end.

3 Pass the tag end of the line behind and around the main line a second time.

4 Then a third time, this time passing the tag end through the center of the circles you made to form a noose.

5 Slide the noose down tightly onto the spool. Then, wind on line until the spool is full.

Hook, line, and sinker

Back to basics Together, these three items are the main elements of what is known as terminal tackle—the business end of your line along with the gear connected to it. It's the bare minimum you need to catch a fish.

HOOKS

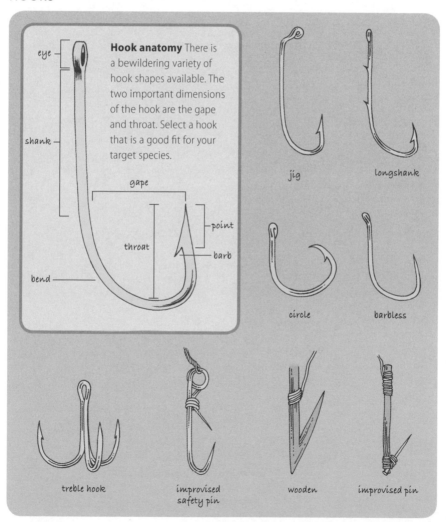

Hook anatomy There is a bewildering variety of hook shapes available. The two important dimensions of the hook are the gape and throat. Select a hook that is a good fit for your target species.

eye

shank

gape

point

throat

barb

bend

jig

longshank

circle

barbless

treble hook

improvised safety pin

wooden

improvised pin

SINKERS

Weigh down low Sinkers are weights, usually made of lead. They provide casting weight for bait-fishing rigs and help position the bait where it has the best chance of attracting fish.

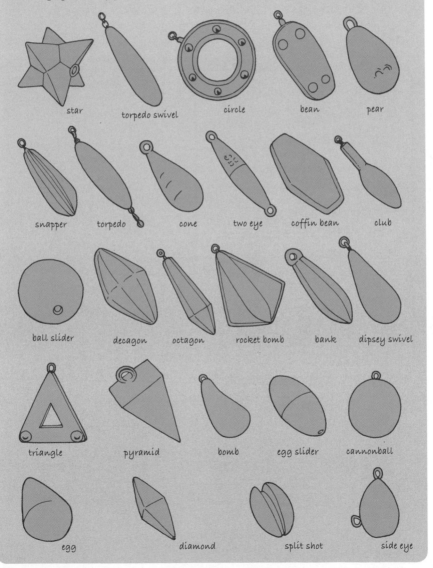

star   torpedo swivel   circle   bean   pear

snapper   torpedo   cone   two eye   coffin bean   club

ball slider   decagon   octagon   rocket bomb   bank   dipsey swivel

triangle   pyramid   bomb   egg slider   cannonball

egg   diamond   split shot   side eye

LINE

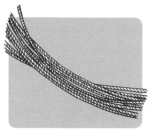

Monofilament The most popular type of fishing line is made from a single strand of slightly stretchy nylon.

Braided These lines have a very high strength-to-diameter ratio and zero stretch providing good "feel" with a hooked fish.

Fly line The line in fly-fishing provides all your casting weight. Some lines float, others sink at a given rate.

OTHER TERMINAL TACKLE

Extras An effective fishing rig often requires more than a hook and sinker at the end of the line. A boom is used to hold a trace line away from the main line. Swivels reduce line twist. Feeders bring fish to your baited hook.

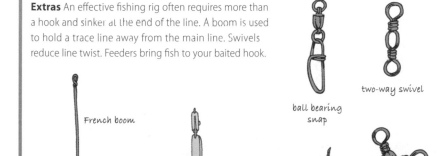

French boom

ball bearing snap

two-way swivel

three-way swivel

split ring for attaching hooks to lures

block end feeder

open end feeder

FLOATS

Surface dwellers Floats are used to suspend bait at depths where fish are feeding. They also give a visual indication of bites—if the float shoots under the surface, twitches, or suddenly lies flat, you have a bite.

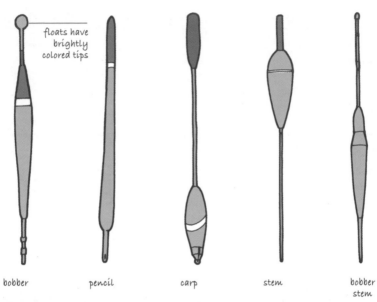

floats have brightly colored tips

bobber   pencil   carp   stem   bobber stem

FLOAT RIGGING

Float and line A float can either be fixed or running. A fixed rig usually has a stopper directly above and below the float, or the line is secured with a clip or rubber band. A running float has a stopper above the float to set the depth the bait is to be presented at.

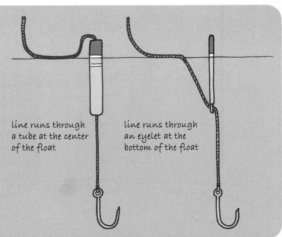

line runs through a tube at the center of the float

line runs through an eyelet at the bottom of the float

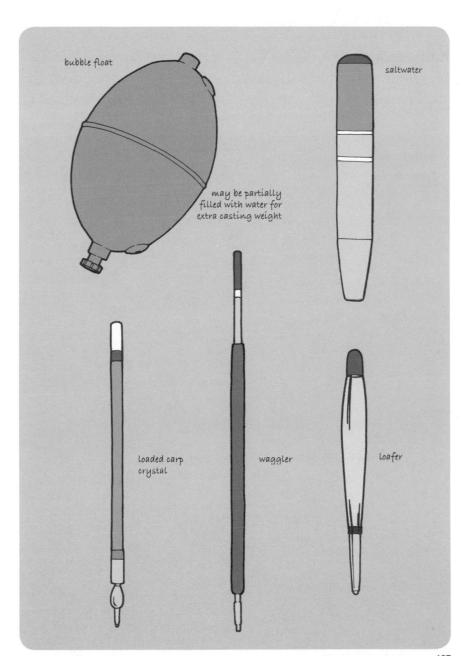

bubble float

saltwater

may be partially
filled with water for
extra casting weight

loaded carp
crystal

waggler

loafer

Fishing knots

Knots to know A knot can make all the difference between landing a big fish or losing it, so it's vital to do them correctly. Fortunately, the average angler needs to master only a few basic knots to be fit for a lifetime of fishing.

BLOOD KNOT

Eye tied Also known as the clinch knot, this is one of the most widely used fishing knots. Use it to attach a line to the eye of a hook, swivel, or lure.

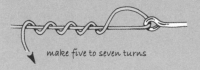

make five to seven turns

1 Pass the line through the eye. Double back and make at least five turns around the line.

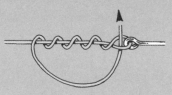

2 Pass the end of the line through the first loop, above the eye.

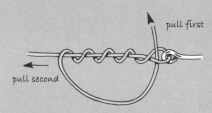

pull first

pull second

3 Lubricate the whole knot with a little saliva. Pull the short end through, and then pull steadily on the other end.

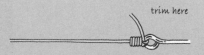

trim here

4 Make sure the coils are in a spiral, not overlapping each other. Slide the coils down tight against the eye, and trim the excess line.

UNI KNOT

Secure and simple The uni knot is a good alternative to the blood knot. It's very reliable and is so simple, you can easily tie it when it's getting dark.

1 Run the line through the eye of the hook, swivel, or lure. Double back parallel to the first line. Make several loops around the double line.

2 Moisten the lines and gently pull the tag end so the knot closes but is not tight.

3 Gently slide the knot up against the eye. Pull both ends until the knot is tight. Finish by trimming the excess line.

SURGEON'S KNOT

Linked lines The surgeon's knot is a quick and effective way to join two lines of unequal diameter. It's frequently used in fly-fishing to attach a tippet to a leader.

1 Lay the two lines alongside each other. Make an overhand knot with both lines. Make a second wrap around the overhand knot.

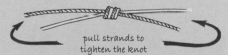

pull strands to tighten the knot

2 With equal pressure on each strand, pull the knot tight. Trim the tag ends.

BAIT

Tasty traps The natural smell and allure of live or fresh bait is irresistible to a foraging fish. Bait can be either purchased or collected, and the possibilities are endless. Experiment and discover what most appeals to your target fish.

FRESHWATER BAIT

Dog biscuits These doggy delicacies will tempt many fish species. Soak and drain the biscuits. Then, place the wet biscuits in an airtight bag and leave for 12 hours or so. After this, they should be rubbery and perfect to hook.

Boilies To make boilies, combine soy flour, animal proteins, fish paste, coloring, and eggs. Roll the mixture into small balls and boil them (hence the name). They should have a hard outer skin to discourage the attention of smaller, unwanted fish.

Corn The natural sweet flavor and bright yellow color of corn is highly attractive to many freshwater fish, especially tench, carp, and bream.

Maggots Live maggots will attract almost any kind of freshwater fish. You can buy maggots from bait shops dead or alive. Fish eat both but are more attracted to live ones. They are often dyed with colorings to enhance their appeal.

Worms A wriggling earthworm on a hook is the all-time classic bait. Collect them by digging in the topsoil or looking under rotting timber in wet areas.

Grasshopper Hook a grasshopper under the hard shell covering the back and shoulders. They are very effective when cast, as you would a fly or lure.

Freshwater shrimp These crustaceans can be caught in a shrimp trap in lakes and streams. Pass the hook through the tail of a large shrimp, or hang several small ones together.

SALTWATER BAIT

Clam Shellfish appeal to a wide variety of fresh- and saltwater fish. You can collect clams and mussels yourself while fishing in shallow waters.

Bread Try hooking a chunk of bread through a tough crust, or squeezing it into a tight ball. Bread can provide a buoyant, sinking, or neutral bait.

Mackerel It's a well-known fact that big fish eat little fish, and the best little fish to use as live bait is probably the mackerel.

Beach worm Fished whole and alive, bunched on a hook, beach worms are very effective for many saltwater species. Catching beach worms is easy with a little practice.

Shrimp Frozen shrimp are a big seller in tackle shops. Extremely fresh or live shrimp are even better.

Squid Cut a large squid into pieces to use as bait. Get rid of the guts and skin—it's the meat that will attract your target fish. Small squid can be hooked whole.

Offal Bird and mammal kidneys, livers, and other smelly odds and ends will tempt many big saltwater fish.

Crab Crabs make excellent bait for beach or rock fishing. Small crabs are best fished as floating bait or on the bottom. Break larger crabs apart and use the meat.

Roe Cured fish eggs are one of the most effective baits for enticing salmon, steelhead, and trout to bite.

Fish meat A fillet or "chunk" of fish meat is a good bait for surf or offshore fishing. Some anglers add a scented product to fish pieces for added attraction.

LURES

Signs of life Lures are artificial baits. Some lures look strikingly similar to the prey of predatory fish, but many unnatural-looking lures rely on movement and vibration, and are very effective.

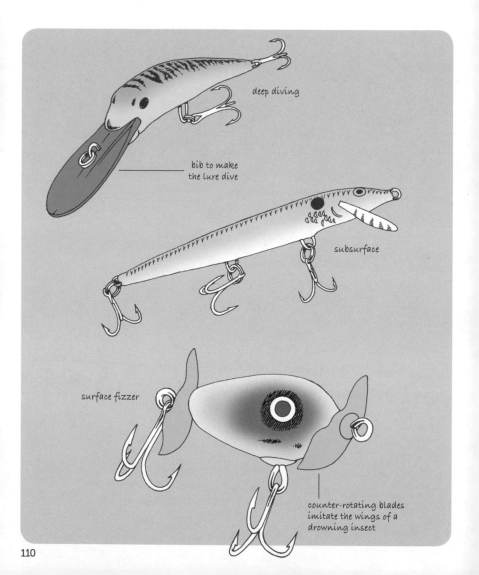

deep diving

bib to make
the lure dive

subsurface

surface fizzer

counter-rotating blades
imitate the wings of a
drowning insect

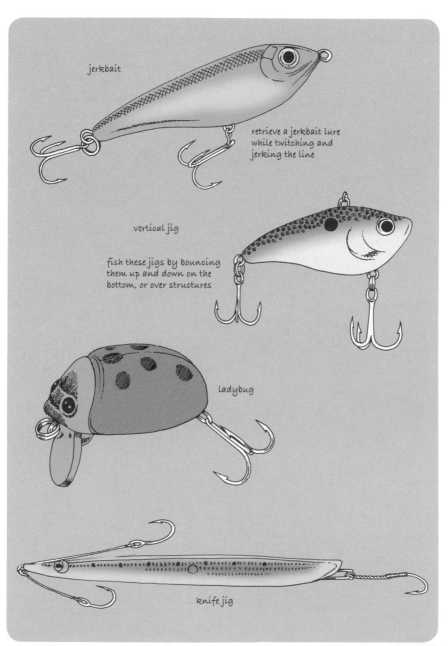

jerkbait

retrieve a jerkbait lure
while twitching and
jerking the line

verticul jig

fish these jigs by bouncing
them up and down on the
bottom, or over structures

ladybug

knife jig

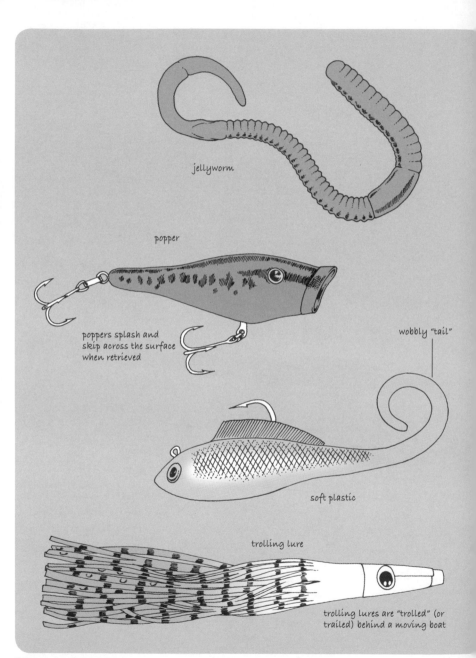

jellyworm

popper

poppers splash and
skip across the surface
when retrieved

wobbly "tail"

soft plastic

trolling lure

trolling lures are "trolled" (or
trailed) behind a moving boat

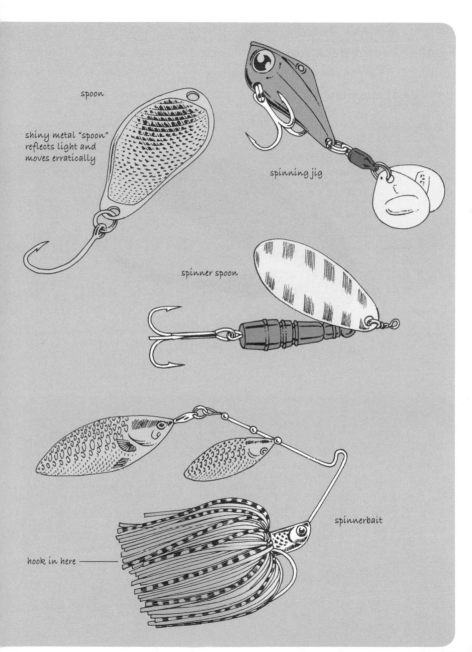

spoon

shiny metal "spoon" reflects light and moves erratically

spinning jig

spinner spoon

spinnerbait

hook in here

Flies

Featherweight deceptors Flies are a specialized type of lure, traditionally constructed from animal fur and bird feathers to create an illusion of life. They are very light and are cast using the weight of the fly line itself.

FLY ANATOMY

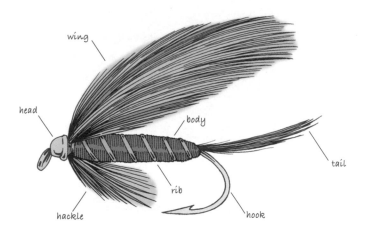

wing

head

body

tail

rib

hackle

hook

FLY TYING KIT

Get creative If you're a keen fly-fisher who wishes to improve your chances of catching fish, fly tying is a most rewarding skill to master. There are many kits on the market to get you started.

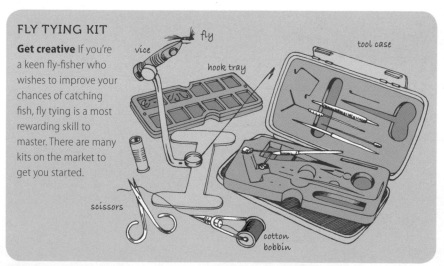

fly

vice

tool case

hook tray

scissors

cotton bobbin

FRESHWATER DRY FLIES

Surface dwellers Dry flies are designed to float on the surface of the water when cast. They mimic adult insects that have fallen into the water, or those that have just hatched on the surface.

Adam's parachute

Chernobyl ant

daddy long legs

F-fly

humpy

mayfly

FRESHWATER WET FLIES

Sinkers A wet fly is designed to sink. They typically mimic a drowned terrestrial insect or a nymph—an insect in the aquatic larval stage of its life. Wet flies may also be made to resemble small fish or other underwater prey.

damsel nymph

coq de Leon & peacock

grizzly king

woolly worm

depth charge Czech mate

hare's ear nymph

SALTWATER FLIES

Ocean snares Saltwater flies are larger than their freshwater equivalents, and normally require heavier tackle rods and reels to handle large, powerful saltwater fish. They typically resemble shrimp, crabs, and small fish.

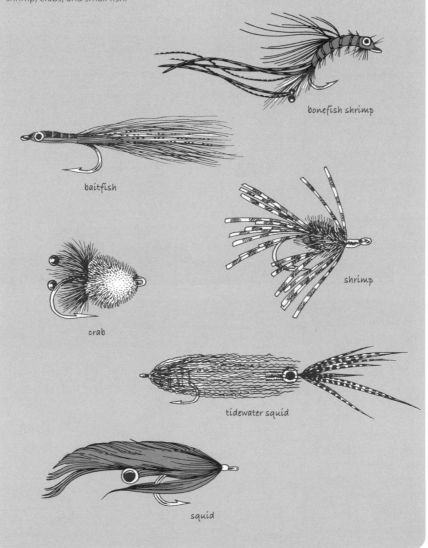

bonefish shrimp

baitfish

shrimp

crab

tidewater squid

squid

FISHING RIGS

Presentation is everything A rig is an arrangement of lines, hooks, sinkers, swivels, floats, and other terminal tackle designed to catch fish. The choice of rig is determined by the target fish and the conditions on the day.

FREELINE

Keep it simple This rig is nothing more than a line and baited hook—simplicity itself! You'll need bait that sinks under its own weight, or has slightly neutral buoyancy. Consider adding a swivel to prevent line twist.

RUNNING FLOAT

Buoyant rig When this rig hits the water, the weight of the sinker and bait will pull the line through the float until the stop is reached. This will position your bait where you suspect that fish are feeding. It can also be used to keep your hook above a snaggy bottom.

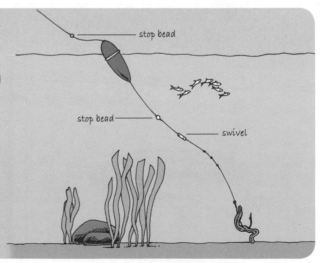

stop bead

stop bead

swivel

RUNNING SINKER

Run free With this rig, the line runs freely through a sinker with an eye or hollow core. A running sinker rig will enable you to present your bait in a much more lifelike manner than having it anchored to the bottom. It also allows the line to be paid out when a fish first picks up the bait.

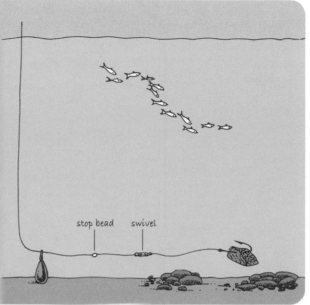

stop bead swivel

PATERNOSTER

Bait in the clear
A paternoster is any style of rig where the main line is anchored by a fixed sinker while the hooks are on short lengths of line—"droppers"—above the sinker. It's a popular rig for ocean shore or deep sea fishing from a boat, but can be adapted to many situations.

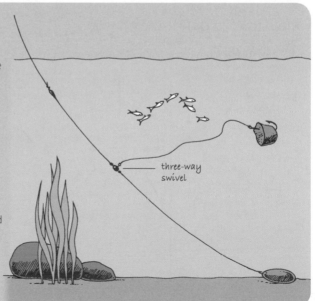

three-way swivel

BEACH BOTTOM

Get down low This rig presents the bait along the sandy bottom— exactly where many species of fish will be feeding. Use the lightest sinker necessary, that way the rig will move with the current.

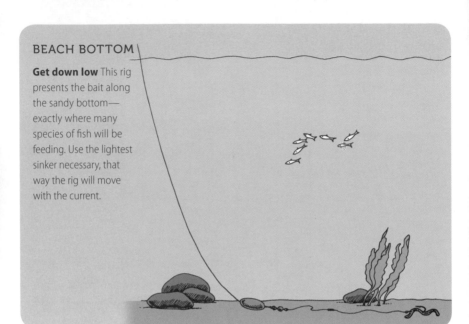

UNWEIGHTED GANG HOOK

Three times lucky A gang hook rig is a set of two or three hooks tied or linked together. When hooked into a baitfish, no sinker will be required. This is a great rig to cast into a school of feeding fish.

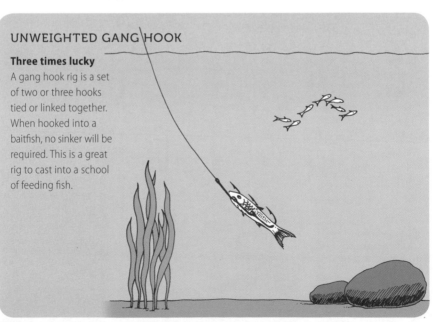

SURFACE

Floating bait A great many baits are best presented on the surface of the water. Baits that float are invariably light. This rig incorporates a bubble float partially filled with water to give casting weight.

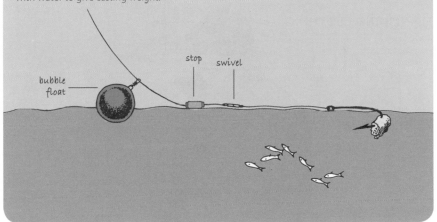

BUOYANT

Suspended bait

Many homemade and commercially available baits are buoyant. Use a length of light line connected to a sinker and swivel to set these baits at a height above the bottom, where fish are feeding.

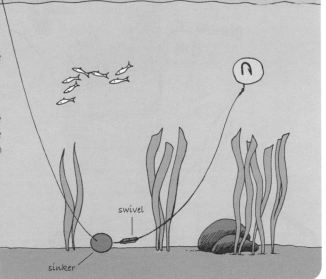

Accessories

Angling extras The smart angler knows how to stay comfortable in the outdoors and is ready to change his or her plan of attack when conditions change. Just a few extra items can mean a much better fishing experience.

FLY-FISHING CLOTHING

cap

polarized sunglasses

waterproof jacket

gloves

waterproof waders

gravel guards to keep stones out of boots

felt-soled wading boots

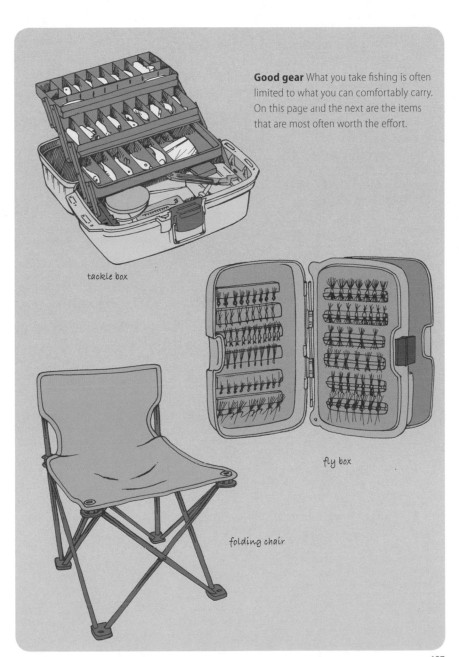

Good gear What you take fishing is often limited to what you can comfortably carry. On this page and the next are the items that are most often worth the effort.

tackle box

fly box

folding chair

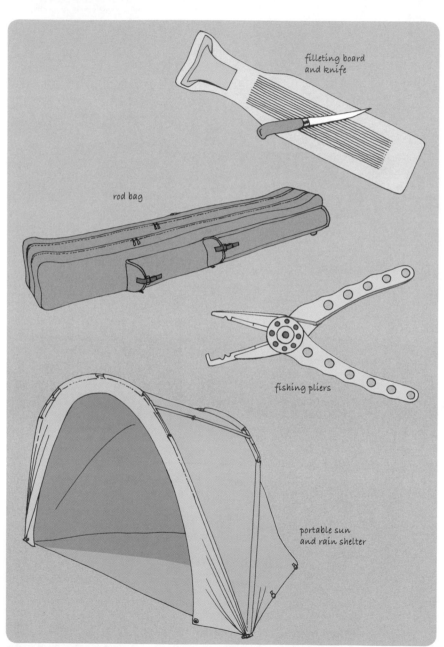

filleting board and knife

rod bag

fishing pliers

portable sun and rain shelter

CASTING

Cast away Casting is the means by which you deliver the bait, lure, or fly to the fish. It takes practice, but once mastered, smooth and accurate casting is one of the definite pleasures of fishing.

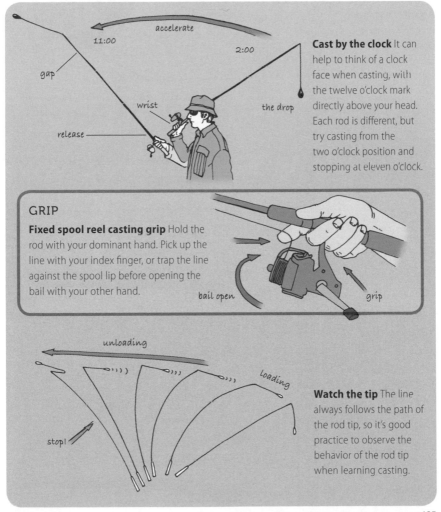

Cast by the clock It can help to think of a clock face when casting, with the twelve o'clock mark directly above your head. Each rod is different, but try casting from the two o'clock position and stopping at eleven o'clock.

GRIP

Fixed spool reel casting grip Hold the rod with your dominant hand. Pick up the line with your index finger, or trap the line against the spool lip before opening the bail with your other hand.

Watch the tip The line always follows the path of the rod tip, so it's good practice to observe the behavior of the rod tip when learning casting.

FLY CAST GRIP

Gently does it Place your thumb on top and slightly to the left of center so that the "V" between the thumb and the index finger is in line with the top of the rod. Hold the rod firmly—but it is a mistake to grip it too hard.

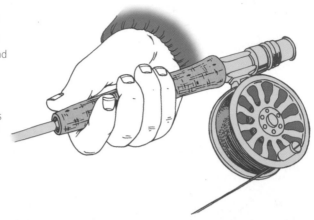

ROLL CAST

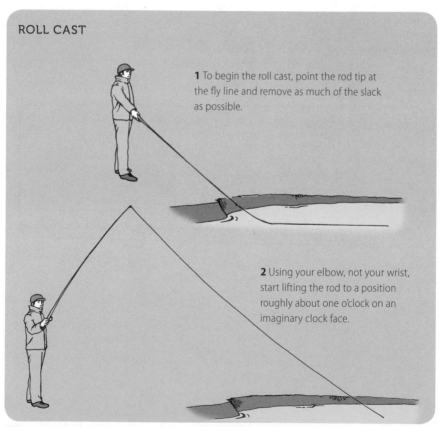

1 To begin the roll cast, point the rod tip at the fly line and remove as much of the slack as possible.

2 Using your elbow, not your wrist, start lifting the rod to a position roughly about one o'clock on an imaginary clock face.

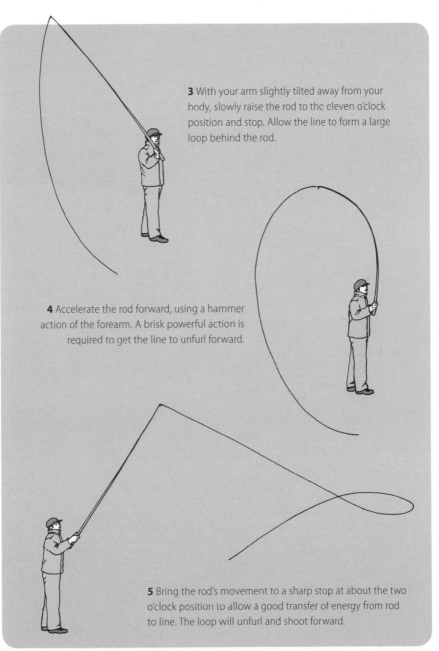

3 With your arm slightly tilted away from your body, slowly raise the rod to the eleven o'clock position and stop. Allow the line to form a large loop behind the rod.

4 Accelerate the rod forward, using a hammer action of the forearm. A brisk powerful action is required to get the line to unfurl forward.

5 Bring the rod's movement to a sharp stop at about the two o'clock position to allow a good transfer of energy from rod to line. The loop will unfurl and shoot forward.

OVERHEAD FLY CAST

1 As with the roll cast, begin with the rod tip pointed at the fly line on the surface of the water. Stand with your right foot forward (if you are right-handed) with knees slightly bent.

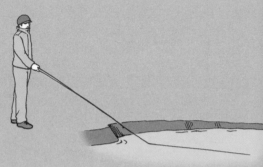

2 Slowly raise the rod to the one o'clock position using your elbow. This will lift the line off the water.

3 Accelerate the action until the rod is raised to a vertical position. Momentum will take the rod back a little to about eleven o'clock. Your hand should be to the side, but just in front of your face. The line should flow upward and then back behind you in a straight line.

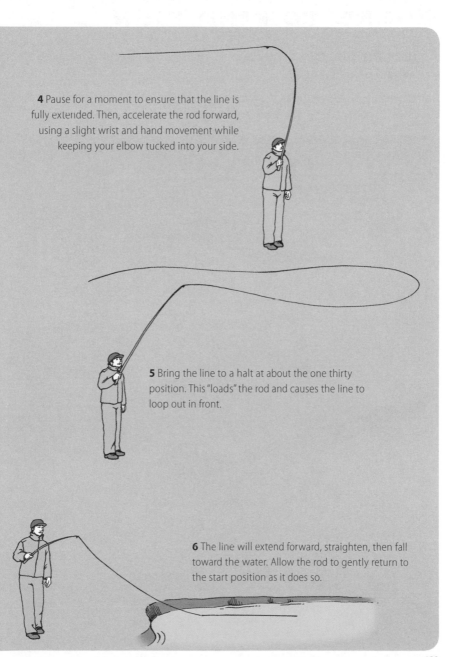

4 Pause for a moment to ensure that the line is fully extended. Then, accelerate the rod forward, using a slight wrist and hand movement while keeping your elbow tucked into your side.

5 Bring the line to a halt at about the one thirty position. This "loads" the rod and causes the line to loop out in front.

6 The line will extend forward, straighten, then fall toward the water. Allow the rod to gently return to the start position as it does so.

WHERE TO FIND FISH

A place for plaice? Just like people, or any other creature, fish tend to congregate in certain places at certain times. Knowing where to fish is the primary factor that separates the successful angler from the fishless.

WHERE IN A STREAM

1. beneath overhanging bushy branches
2. undercut river bend
3. still water
4. feeder stream joining main stream
5. calm water behind rocks
6. beneath dead tree in water

LAKE BREEZES

Ripple effect On a breezy day, observe where the wind is blowing the surface of the water. Leeward shorelines and points will be rich with trapped insects and even baitfish, which in turn will attract larger fish.

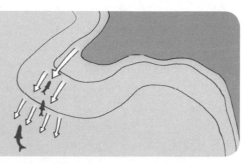

LAKE INLETS

Water flow Fish will congregate where a river or stream enters a lake—they like the oxygenated water and the food that it brings. They will also gather where there is outgoing water.

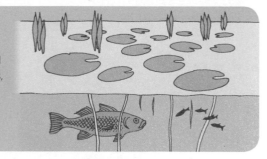

LAKE LILY PADS

In the shade Lily pads are rich with aquatic life, which attract baitfish, and baitfish attract larger fish. On hot days, fish will also seek the shade that lily pads provide.

LAKE CLIFF

Rough descent Fish congregate wherever there is structure underwater. A rugged cliff or steep shore bank will offer many places to feed, hide, and spawn.

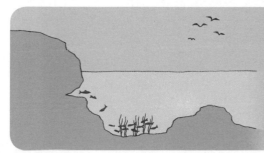

LAKE PIER

Fish underfoot Piers and docks provide shelter and shade for fish, and an abundance of food associated with the weeds and barnacles that grow on them.

LAKE WEED BEDS

Weedy bottom Weed beds are an important habitat for small fish and the game fish that hunt them. Look for weed beds that lead to deeper water.

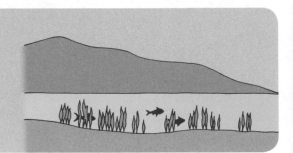

LAKE ROCKS

Stony shelter Rocks provide food, shelter, shade, and a place to spawn. The best rock formations are those that come from deep water close to the surface.

LAKE SUNKEN OBJECT

Fish wreck Sunken objects, such as logs, branches, stumps, and boats, all provide structure. Take care not to get snagged, and be very careful around sunken objects if you are in a boat.

BAY CHANNEL

Find the current Anywhere that water is forced into a narrow opening, there will be a strong current and a concentration of food. A channel between two islands is ideal.

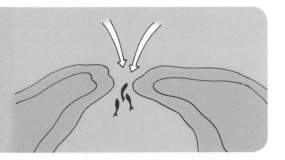

BAY LEAPING FISH

Fish out of water If you see small fish leaping out of the water, they are probably being hunted by larger fish. Cast your bait or lure into the area.

BAY BIRDS

Signs from above Birds circling around and diving into water are a sure sign of baitfish. There are likely to be bigger fish hunting under the surface.

BAY TIDAL MUD FLATS

Tide is high When the tide is high and intertidal mud flats become submerged, fish will move in to feed on crabs, mollusks, and worms.

SHORE OUTLET

Mouth of the river Wherever a river, bay, or estuary discharges into the ocean, there is likely to be a rich flow of food and large saltwater fish species.

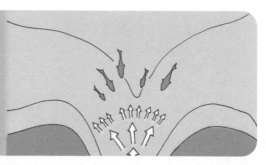

SHORE POINT

Good point Points that project into the ocean are associated with strong currents that create deep channels and shallow sandbanks, where big and small fish dwell. They also create an obstacle where game fish can corral baitfish.

SHORE DEEP WATER

Deep water big fish Look for places where deep water comes close to shore. These can give access to game fish that can normally be caught only from a boat.

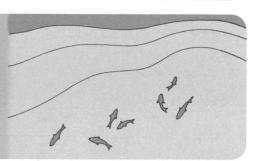

SHORE GUTTER

Rip tide Water that crashes to the beach in waves usually returns via rip currents that cut a "gutter" close to shore and running parallel to it. Fish face into the current in these gutters, harvesting food washed into them.

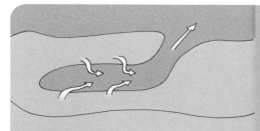

SHORE FISH SCHOOL

Follow the minnows Look for disturbances in the surface, baitfish jumping, or birds circling overhead. Where baitfish go, so do the fish you want to catch.

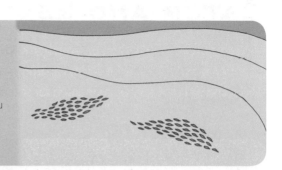

SHORE SEAWALL

Fish stop Many game fish use artificial seawalls as dead-end surfaces to entrap prey they have driven in from adjacent docks or deeper channels. It's better to drop your bait straight down off a seawall than to cast out.

SHORE CLIFF

Cliff base Below a sea cliff, the underwater landscape is almost invariably eroded and broken—the sort of environment that all fish love.

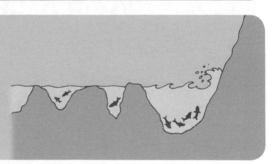

SHORE WEED PATCH

Seaweed Keep an eye out for weed beds and rock piles with weeds attached to them. Smaller fish feed on the weeds and the creatures that live among them, and attract larger fish.

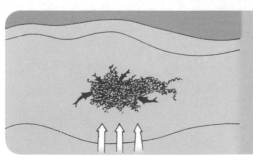

CATCH AND RELEASE

Please release me A fish on your hook doesn't have to end up on your plate. Catch and release fishing plays an important part in conserving fishing stocks, and will probably be mandated for some fish that you catch.

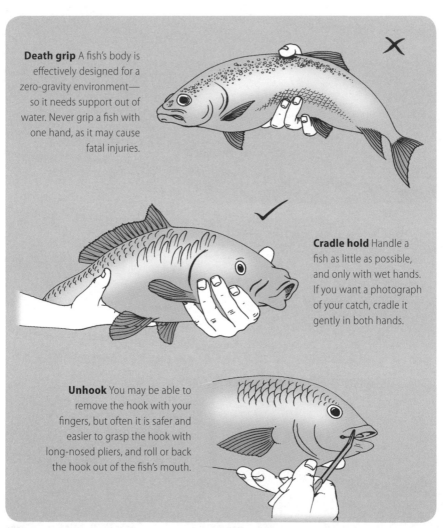

Death grip A fish's body is effectively designed for a zero-gravity environment—so it needs support out of water. Never grip a fish with one hand, as it may cause fatal injuries.

Cradle hold Handle a fish as little as possible, and only with wet hands. If you want a photograph of your catch, cradle it gently in both hands.

Unhook You may be able to remove the hook with your fingers, but often it is safer and easier to grasp the hook with long-nosed pliers, and roll or back the hook out of the fish's mouth.

FISH RELEASE

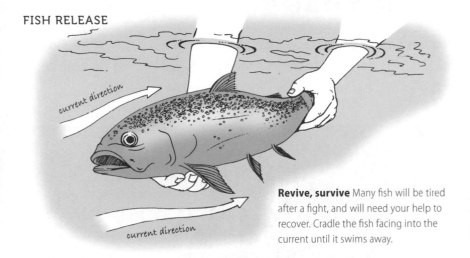

Revive, survive Many fish will be tired after a fight, and will need your help to recover. Cradle the fish facing into the current until it swims away.

HOOKED YOURSELF?—STRING YANK METHOD

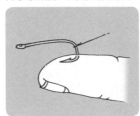

1 Tie some thread or fishing line around the midpoint of the bend in the fishhook.

2 Rotate the shank until it's parallel to the underlying skin. Maintain this pressure.

3 Apply a quick yank to the thread parallel to the shank. Keep clear of the hook.

PUSH-THROUGH METHOD

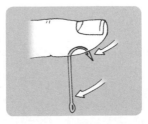

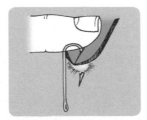

1 A deeply embedded hook will need a different approach that requires a little courage.

2 Firmly push the end of the hook down until the barb completely exits the skin.

3 Cut off the barb. Then, rotate the hook back out through the entry wound.

FISH TRAPS

No way out If you're not so eager to fight it out with a fish on the end of a line, but still want a fish for dinner, it's time to build a fish trap. They can be very effective, and keep your fish fresh while you do other things.

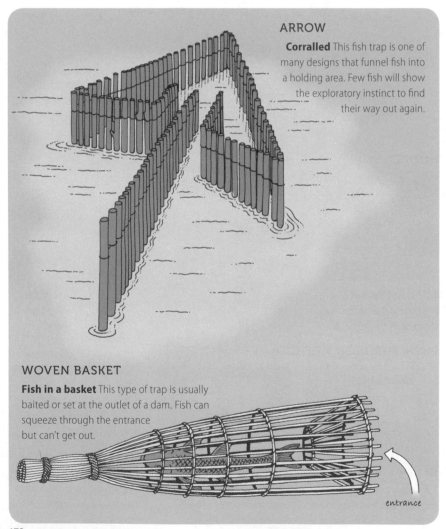

ARROW

Corralled This fish trap is one of many designs that funnel fish into a holding area. Few fish will show the exploratory instinct to find their way out again.

WOVEN BASKET

Fish in a basket This type of trap is usually baited or set at the outlet of a dam. Fish can squeeze through the entrance but can't get out.

entrance

TIDAL

Tidal beach trap Build a curved rock wall just underwater at high tide. Bait it with crushed sea snails or crabs and collect your catch a few hours later.

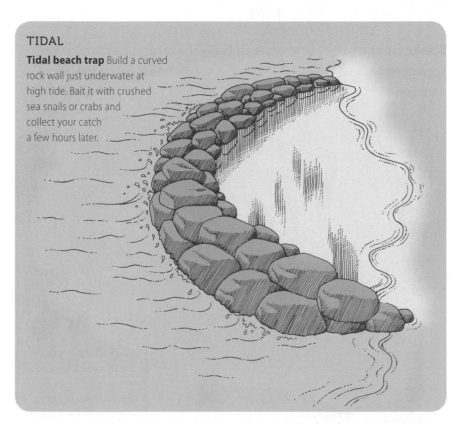

RIVER DAM

Dead end If fish are traveling down a shallow river, block their way with some well-placed stones.

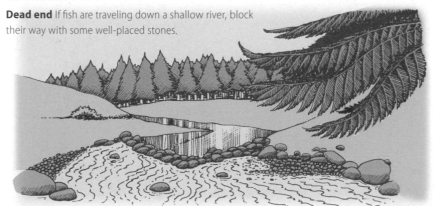

OTHER METHODS

Spear or scoop Spearfishing is probably the original way to hunt fish. Spearguns have their devotees, but the old-style spears still do the job. Alternatively, try bagging a fish with a net—or even your bare hands.

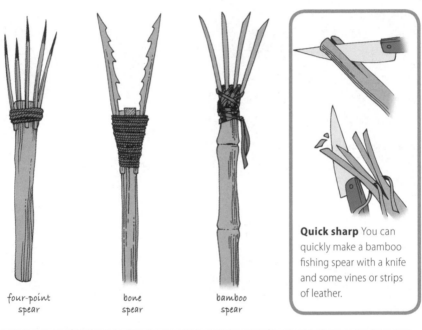

four-point spear

bone spear

bamboo spear

Quick sharp You can quickly make a bamboo fishing spear with a knife and some vines or strips of leather.

REFRACTION

Aim off target When light passes from the air to the water, or water to the air, it is bent, or refracted. Make allowances for this by throwing your spear at a spot a bit closer than the fish appears to be.

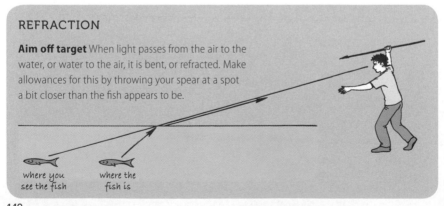

where you see the fish

where the fish is

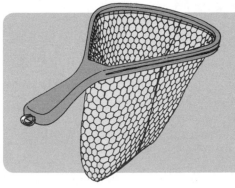

NET

It's a scoop Use a net where fish are visible. To catch a fish, first place the net in the water so you can get a proper alignment (see "Refraction," opposite). Move the net slowly or the fish may be frightened off. When the net is close enough, quickly scoop it out of the water.

ICE FISHING

Dinner under ice Cut a hole (or several if possible) over the deepest part of a frozen lake. Set up an automatic fisherman and wait for a bite. Stay off any ice less than four inches thick. Clear blue ice is the strongest.

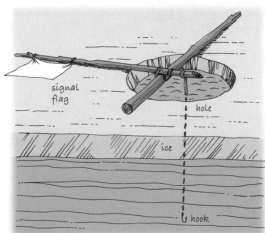

CATCH A FISH BAREHANDED

1 Reach under a riverbank into deep, slow-moving water. Allow your arm to reach water temperature.

2 Slowly move your hands until you touch a fish. Lightly tickle its underbelly, which will lull the fish into complacency.

3 Work your hands along the fish's belly until you reach its gills. In one motion, catapult the fish out of the water.

PREPARING FISH

Kill and cook For many anglers, a fish on a plate is the supreme way to finish off a day by the water. If you've caught a fish that you plan on eating, there are a few things that need doing first.

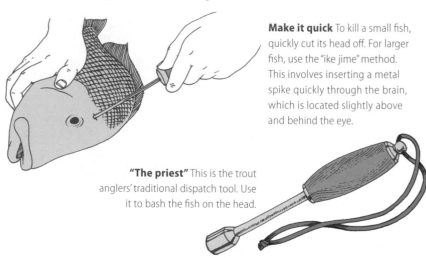

Make it quick To kill a small fish, quickly cut its head off. For larger fish, use the "ike jime" method. This involves inserting a metal spike quickly through the brain, which is located slightly above and behind the eye.

"The priest" This is the trout anglers' traditional dispatch tool. Use it to bash the fish on the head.

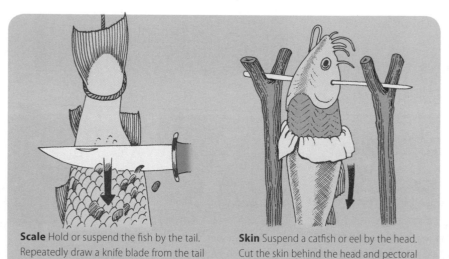

Scale Hold or suspend the fish by the tail. Repeatedly draw a knife blade from the tail to the head. The scales will start to roll off.

Skin Suspend a catfish or eel by the head. Cut the skin behind the head and pectoral fins. Draw the skin down toward the tail.

FILLET A SMALL FISH

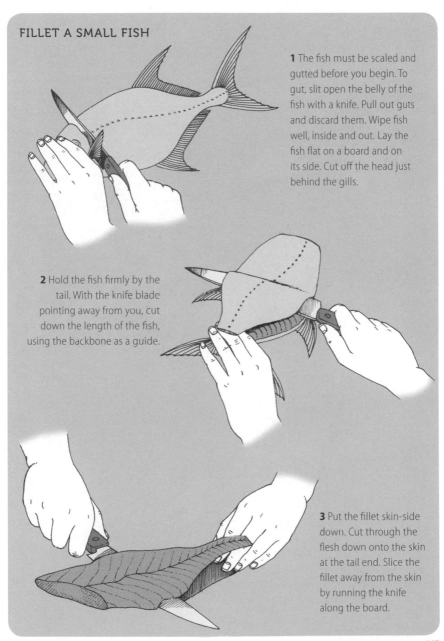

1 The fish must be scaled and gutted before you begin. To gut, slit open the belly of the fish with a knife. Pull out guts and discard them. Wipe fish well, inside and out. Lay the fish flat on a board and on its side. Cut off the head just behind the gills.

2 Hold the fish firmly by the tail. With the knife blade pointing away from you, cut down the length of the fish, using the backbone as a guide.

3 Put the fillet skin-side down. Cut through the flesh down onto the skin at the tail end. Slice the fillet away from the skin by running the knife along the board.

FILLET A LARGE FISH

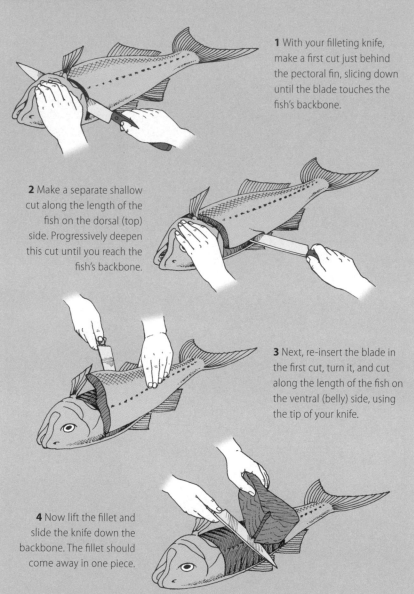

1 With your filleting knife, make a first cut just behind the pectoral fin, slicing down until the blade touches the fish's backbone.

2 Make a separate shallow cut along the length of the fish on the dorsal (top) side. Progressively deepen this cut until you reach the fish's backbone.

3 Next, re-insert the blade in the first cut, turn it, and cut along the length of the fish on the ventral (belly) side, using the tip of your knife.

4 Now lift the fillet and slide the knife down the backbone. The fillet should come away in one piece.

COOKING FISH

Dinnertime It's important not to overcook fish, as this makes the flesh tough and destroys flavor. It is difficult to tell when fish is cooked by looking at it. One method is to check with a fork—if the flesh is still solid or if it will break apart under light pressure from the fork.

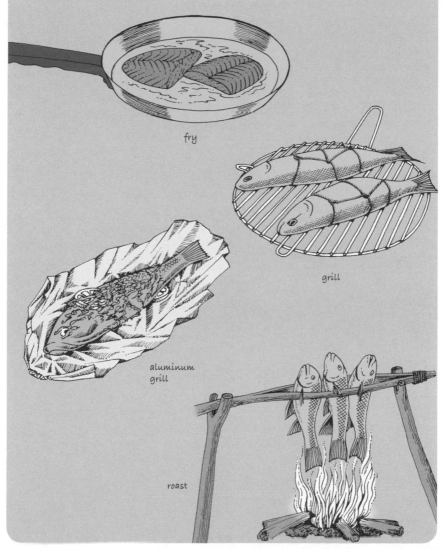

fry

grill

aluminum grill

roast

CLIMBING

There are many forms of climbing: alpine, sport, traditional, aid, solo, mountaineering, and bouldering. At their heart is a love of the outdoors and an ability to move up, using foot- and hand-holds or climbing gear.

Rock-climbing gear

Moving up To the uninitiated, climbing equipment can be bamboozling. However, it really just consists of a harness and ropes (to hold the climber if they fall), special rubber-soled shoes, and devices to clip the rope into.

BASIC KIT

Climb when ready
Equipment is attached to the harness and, in hot or sweaty conditions, a bag of gymnasts' chalk is often hung on the back of the harness to help you maintain grip.

warm shell layer

rope

quickdraw carabiners

belay gloves

clothes that allow movement

chalk bag

thin-soled climbing shoes

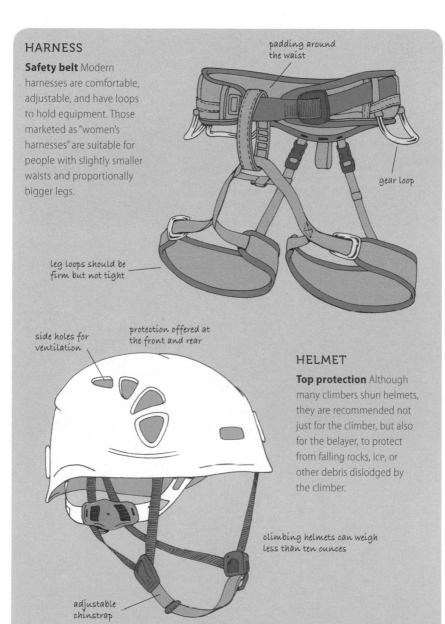

HARNESS

Safety belt Modern harnesses are comfortable, adjustable, and have loops to hold equipment. Those marketed as "women's harnesses" are suitable for people with slightly smaller waists and proportionally bigger legs.

padding around the waist

gear loop

leg loops should be firm but not tight

side holes for ventilation

protection offered at the front and rear

HELMET

Top protection Although many climbers shun helmets, they are recommended not just for the climber, but also for the belayer, to protect from falling rocks, ice, or other debris dislodged by the climber.

climbing helmets can weigh less than ten ounces

adjustable chinstrap

HIGH SHOE

All-arounder With heel protection and a flat sole suitable for "smearing" a large area of the foot on smooth slabs, these are a comfortable, all-around climbing shoe.

LOW SHOE

Aggressive A high arch and a toe that comes down to a point makes this style of shoe perfect for standing on the tiniest crinkle in the rock.

SLIPPER

Convenient Climbers who mainly do short, intense sporty climbs often find slippers more convenient, as they are frequently pulling their tight-fitting shoes on and off.

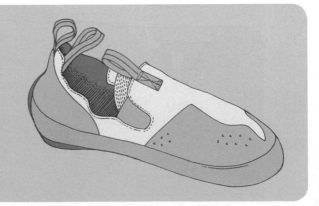

ROCK-CLIMBING EQUIPMENT

Light work When used correctly, rock-climbing equipment—although light—is made to withstand the force of a heavy fall. Most climbers start with a few pieces of basic equipment and add gear as necessary.

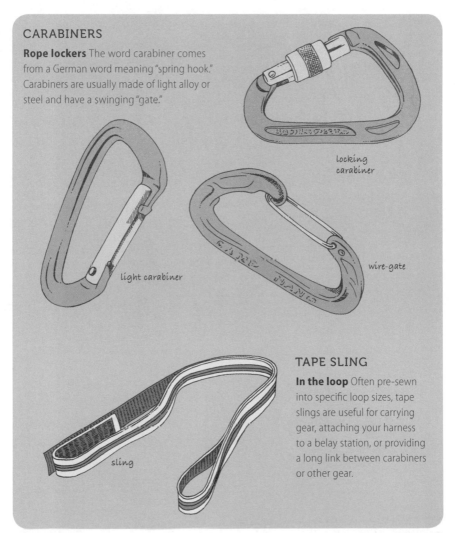

CARABINERS

Rope lockers The word carabiner comes from a German word meaning "spring hook." Carabiners are usually made of light alloy or steel and have a swinging "gate."

locking carabiner

light carabiner

wire-gate

TAPE SLING

In the loop Often pre-sewn into specific loop sizes, tape slings are useful for carrying gear, attaching your harness to a belay station, or providing a long link between carabiners or other gear.

sling

DESCENDERS AND ASCENDERS

Going down In order to safely descend cliffs—to start or finish an expedition, for rescue, or during the middle of a large climb—rock climbers use a variety of rappelling, or descending, devices. Ascenders grip the rope, allowing a climber to safely climb up a rope.

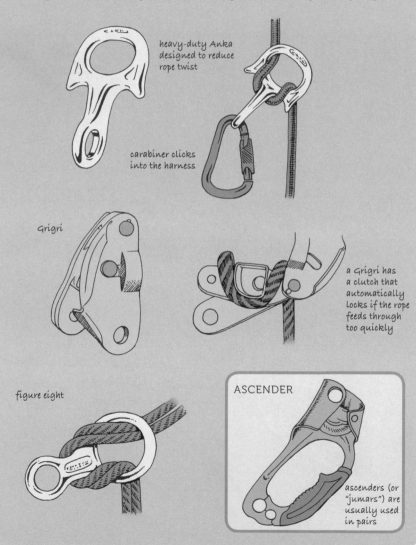

heavy-duty Anka designed to reduce rope twist

carabiner clicks into the harness

Grigri

a Grigri has a clutch that automatically locks if the rope feeds through too quickly

figure eight

ASCENDER

ascenders (or "jumars") are usually used in pairs

BELAY DEVICES

Catch me While one person climbs, another usually belays them—controlling the amount of slack rope and staying ready to arrest a fall. By restricting rope slippage, a belay device makes this easier.

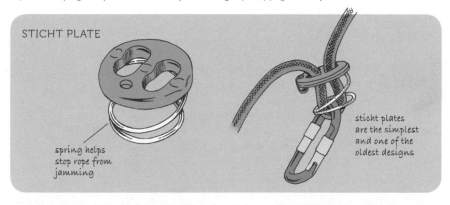

STICHT PLATE

spring helps
stop rope from
jamming

sticht plates
are the simplest
and one of the
oldest designs

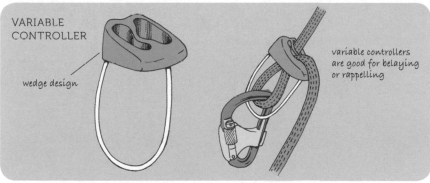

VARIABLE
CONTROLLER

wedge design

variable controllers
are good for belaying
or rappelling

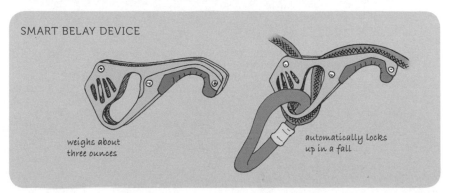

SMART BELAY DEVICE

weighs about
three ounces

automatically locks
up in a fall

PROTECTION DEVICES

The nuts and bolts When lead climbing, a person will place equipment—collectively called "protection"— into rock cracks and crevices, then will clip their rope into it using a carabiner. Some of the simplest forms of protection are "nuts" or "wires," which come in different sizes.

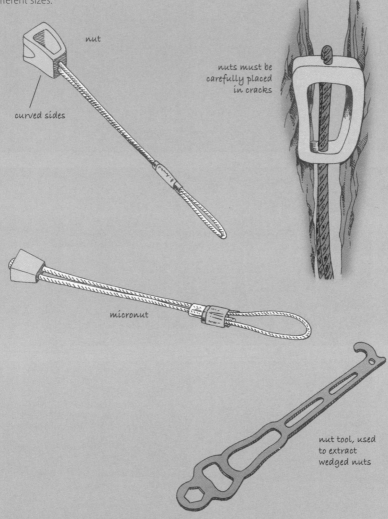

nut

curved sides

nuts must be carefully placed in cracks

micronut

nut tool, used to extract wedged nuts

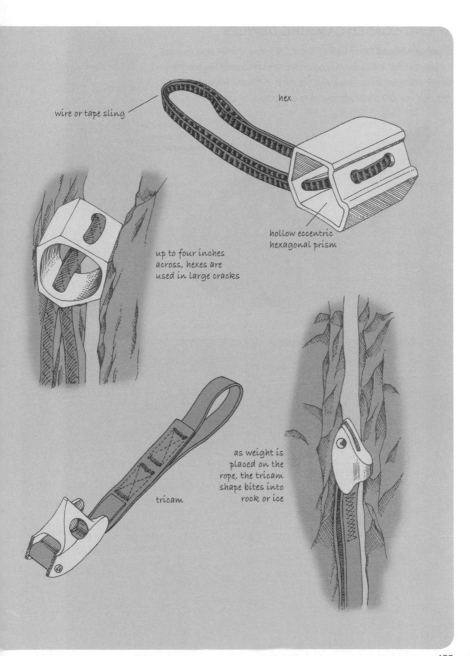

wire or tape sling

hex

hollow eccentric hexagonal prism

up to four inches across, hexes are used in large cracks

as weight is placed on the rope, the tricam shape bites into rock or ice

tricam

SPRING-LOADED CAMMING DEVICES

Climber's friend Often called "friends" or "cams," these devices were invented in the 1970s. By pulling on the spring-loaded trigger, the device collapses quite small, and once it is in place, the spring is released and the teeth pop out to grip a groove or crevice.

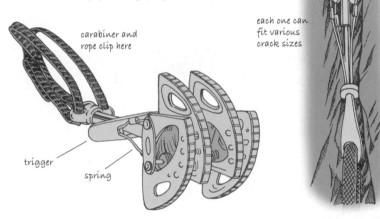

carabiner and
rope clip here

each one can
fit various
crack sizes

trigger

spring

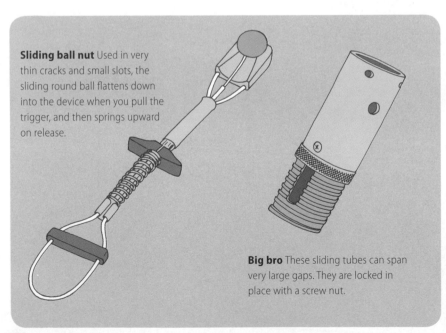

Sliding ball nut Used in very thin cracks and small slots, the sliding round ball flattens down into the device when you pull the trigger, and then springs upward on release.

Big bro These sliding tubes can span very large gaps. They are locked in place with a screw nut.

156

FIXED EQUIPMENT

Pitons Alpine climbers, and those doing "aid climbing," sometimes use more permanent protection, such as pitons, which are hammered into the rock, and expansion bolts, which are drilled and screwed in place. Placing fixed gear is illegal in some areas.

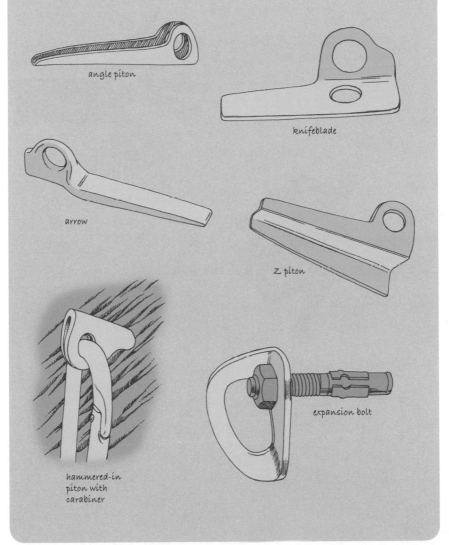

angle piton

knifeblade

arrow

z piton

hammered-in
piton with
carabiner

expansion bolt

Ropes and knots

Life line Climbing ropes can be "static" (meaning they don't stretch) or dynamic, resulting in less load on the rope if you fall. Today's ropes tend to have a diameter of approximately 0.3–0.5 inches.

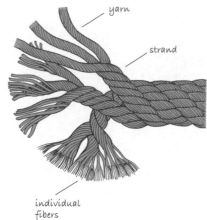

yarn

strand

Laid rope The traditional rope in many outdoor activities, laid rope has three or more strands twisted around each other.

individual fibers

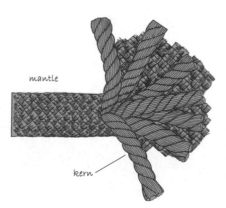

mantle

kern

Kernmantle rope Many modern climbing ropes have a separate protective sheath, or mantle, covering the core fibers.

DAMAGED ROPES

Retirement time The sheath of kernmantle ropes can hide a damaged core. Bulges in the core or tears in the sheath signify it's time for a new rope.

damaged core

damaged sheath

BUTTERFLY COIL

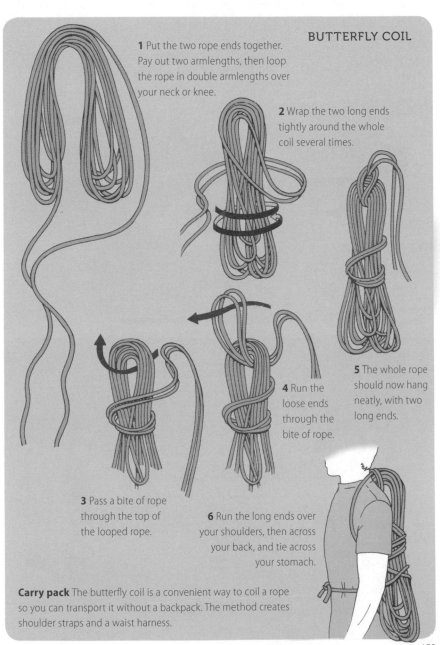

1 Put the two rope ends together. Pay out two armlengths, then loop the rope in double armlengths over your neck or knee.

2 Wrap the two long ends tightly around the whole coil several times.

3 Pass a bite of rope through the top of the looped rope.

4 Run the loose ends through the bite of rope.

5 The whole rope should now hang neatly, with two long ends.

6 Run the long ends over your shoulders, then across your back, and tie across your stomach.

Carry pack The butterfly coil is a convenient way to coil a rope so you can transport it without a backpack. The method creates shoulder straps and a waist harness.

OVERHAND LOOP

Quick and easy One of the quickest ways to make a fixed loop in a rope is the overhand loop, suitable for a quick secure on a belay station. However, this knot can jam tight, and is not considered the best knot for many climbing purposes.

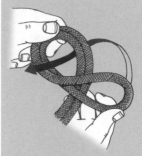  

1 Stretch the loop out over the top of the trailing rope.

2 Put the loop through the created hole.

3 Attach the loop to a carabiner.

FIGURE EIGHT LOOP

More secure Although a bulkier knot, this is considered one of the most secure ways to create a loop in a rope, and is suitable for many climbing purposes.

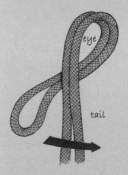  

1 Take a looped bite of rope right around the double "tail."

2 Push the bite up through the original "eye."

3 The finished knot should look a little like an "8."

THREADED FIGURE EIGHT

Secure tie-in This should end up looking the same as the figure eight loop knot, but allows you to tie in to a fixed point, such as a harness or sling. It is done in two parts.

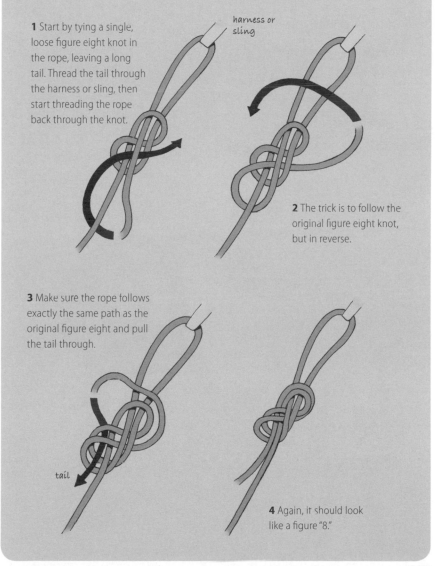

1 Start by tying a single, loose figure eight knot in the rope, leaving a long tail. Thread the tail through the harness or sling, then start threading the rope back through the knot.

harness or sling

2 The trick is to follow the original figure eight knot, but in reverse.

3 Make sure the rope follows exactly the same path as the original figure eight and pull the tail through.

tail

4 Again, it should look like a figure "8."

CLOVE HITCH

Firm and easy Wonderfully simple, quick, and easy to adjust, this hitch is ideal on belay stations. It holds firm in most instances, but can slip if subject to a sudden, heavy load.

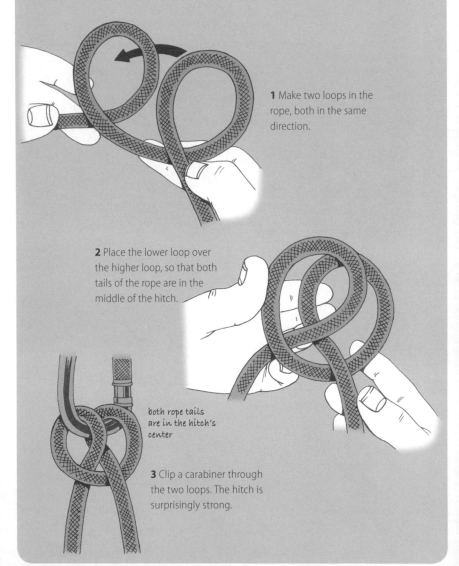

1 Make two loops in the rope, both in the same direction.

2 Place the lower loop over the higher loop, so that both tails of the rope are in the middle of the hitch.

both rope tails are in the hitch's center

3 Clip a carabiner through the two loops. The hitch is surprisingly strong.

ITALIAN HITCH

Emergency belay This hitch increases the amount of friction on the rope, but allows it to slip, so is good for lowering gear, or as an alternative to a belay or rappelling device.

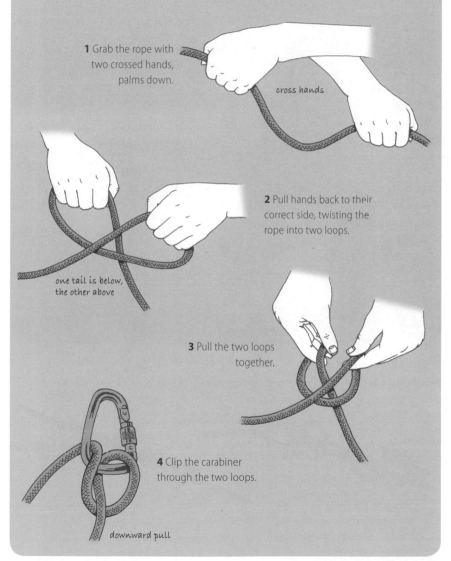

1 Grab the rope with two crossed hands, palms down.

cross hands

2 Pull hands back to their correct side, twisting the rope into two loops.

one tail is below, the other above

3 Pull the two loops together.

4 Clip the carabiner through the two loops.

downward pull

PRUSIK

Nonslip rope The prusik knot is an excellent way to attach a weight to a rope. It slides up and down the rope when unweighted, but doesn't slip under a downward force. Two prusik knots (one for feet, one clipped into the harness) are often used to ascend or "prusik" a rope.

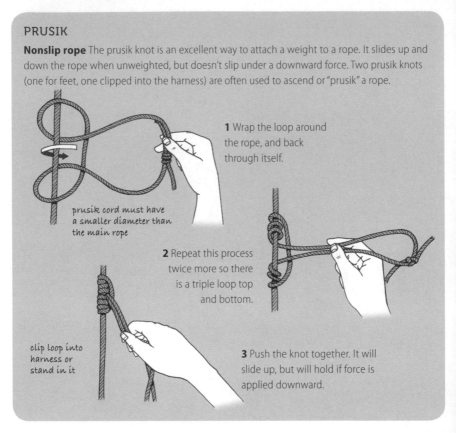

1 Wrap the loop around the rope, and back through itself.

prusik cord must have a smaller diameter than the main rope

2 Repeat this process twice more so there is a triple loop top and bottom.

clip loop into harness or stand in it

3 Push the knot together. It will slide up, but will hold if force is applied downward.

DOUBLE FISHERMAN'S

Two become one This is one of the best knots to securely tie two ropes together, and is useful on long descents. Start by laying the last three feet of each rope alongside each other, tails in opposite directions.

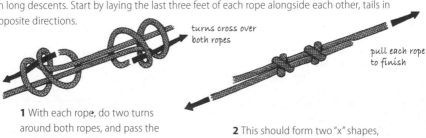

turns cross over both ropes

pull each rope to finish

1 With each rope, do two turns around both ropes, and pass the end back through the loops, away from the knot's center.

2 This should form two "x" shapes, which will then slide together as you pull each rope.

HOLDS AND MOVES

Vertical dance Skilled rock climbers move gracefully and carefully up a rock face, using coordinated hand, finger, foot, and body moves. It requires strength, stamina, agility, and balance.

HANDHOLDS

Jug A large, easily gripped hold around which you can wrap your whole hand.

Crimp A small ledge or feature on which only the finger ends fit.

Thumb pinch Fingers and thumb grip the feature by pinching it.

HANDHOLDS

Finger pinch Sometimes only one finger can be used opposite the thumb.

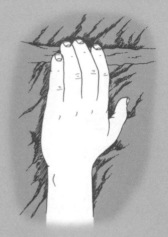

Pull A thin ledge or feature on which a climber can pull themselves up.

Side pull Can be very useful when combined with moving feet up the wall.

Finger hold Usually the second or third digit is used if only one finger will fit.

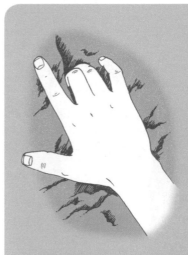

Two-finger hold Sometimes only the smaller fingers will fit.

Finger jam Like a piece of protection, a finger or two is wedged in place.

Hand jam The thumb points down as the hand is inserted and twisted until it jams.

Thumbs up The thumb wedges the back of the hand against the rock.

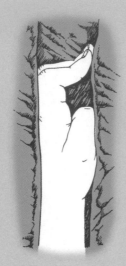

Finger bridge Useful as the crack widens beyond hand height.

Fist jam Clench tight to use the fleshy part of your hand.

Double hand jam As the crack widens beyond a fist, two hands are needed.

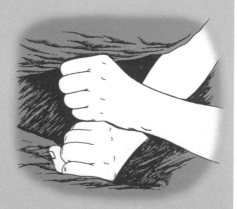

Two fists Relatively secure, this can bridge a wider gap.

FOOTWORK

On your toes Different techniques and parts of the foot are employed, depending on the features and slope of the rock.

Edging A small part of the shoe near the toe is placed carefully on a tiny hold.

Smearing A large amount of the sole is placed in contact with the rock.

Foot jam By twisting the foot into a crack, a secure foothold is obtained.

Heel hook The back of the foot is used to help pull the body upward.

MOVING ON ROCK

Mantle Often needed to finish a climb or to get onto a large rock shelf, the mantle is a technique that involves transferring from a pulling position to a pushing position, and then, with careful balance, standing up. It is usually easier done with momentum in a fluid motion.

1 Palms face down near the edge, pull up using high footholds.

2 As your center of gravity rises, push up onto one side.

3 Cock both elbows, as if doing a push-up, and rock your weight over your palms.

4 Swing a foot up onto the ledge and push through until you are standing.

Layback One of the most stylish and pleasant climbing techniques, the layback matches two opposing forces: the arms pulling away from an edge, and the feet pushing.

Bridging With both legs on opposing walls pushing out, wide gaps on vertical walls can be "bridged." This technique is simple to practice in doorways.

CHIMNEY MEDIUM

1 Brace across the gap, using your legs to push your lower back against the opposite side.

2 Straighten the lower leg, sliding your back up the wall.

3 Move your lower foot to a higher position and repeat.

Chimney wide Alternate bridging with your legs and arms, marching your feet or hands up the wall each time they are free. This technique is strenuous and requires strong abdominal and chest muscles.

Chimney narrow Use any combination of body parts pushing on opposing walls to stabilize and move up. For example, knees opposing feet and bottom, then feet and hands opposing back. Progress can be slow.

BELAYS AND PITCHES

Going up In most traditional forms of climbing, one climber is protected from a fall by the belayer. The belayer's position needs to be secure.

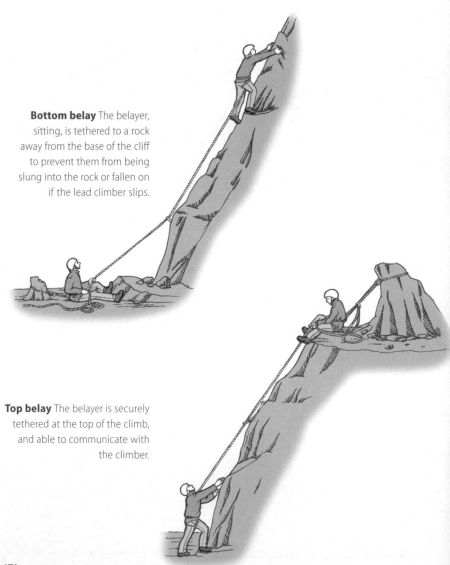

Bottom belay The belayer, sitting, is tethered to a rock away from the base of the cliff to prevent them from being slung into the rock or fallen on if the lead climber slips.

Top belay The belayer is securely tethered at the top of the climb, and able to communicate with the climber.

SINGLE PITCH

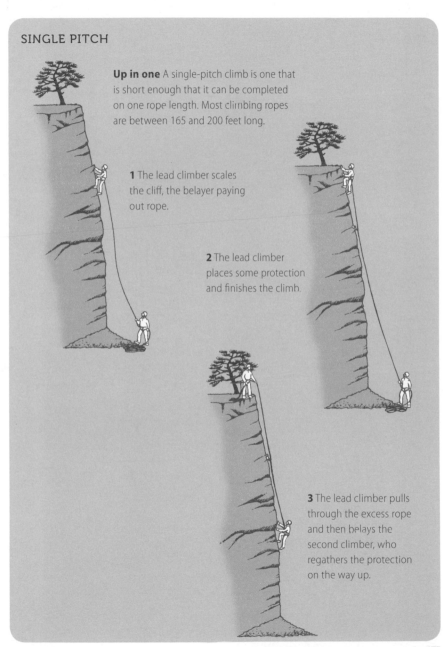

Up in one A single-pitch climb is one that is short enough that it can be completed on one rope length. Most climbing ropes are between 165 and 200 feet long.

1 The lead climber scales the cliff, the belayer paying out rope.

2 The lead climber places some protection and finishes the climb.

3 The lead climber pulls through the excess rope and then belays the second climber, who regathers the protection on the way up.

MULTI PITCH

Big walls If a climb is longer than the length of one rope (usually 165 feet), then the climbers will need to establish belay stations as they go, completing the climb in several "pitches." Big walls may have dozens of pitches.

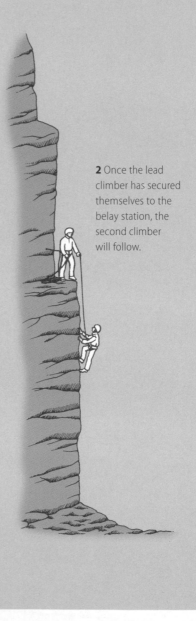

2 Once the lead climber has secured themselves to the belay station, the second climber will follow.

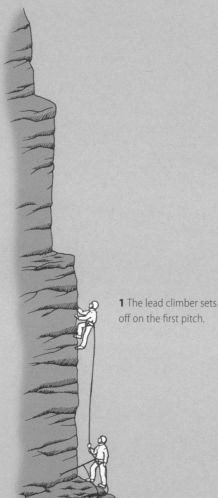

1 The lead climber sets off on the first pitch.

4 This process is repeated until all the pitches are completed. Whoever climbs second usually gathers all the equipment as they go.

3 The second climber may then continue past the belay station, completing the next pitch. Alternatively, the second climber will secure themselves at the belay station, and the lead climber will set out again.

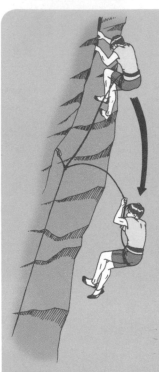

Protecting a fall If a climber falls, they will plummet at least twice as far as their distance to the last piece of protection. On an overhang, this will usually leave them hanging in free space.

Multiple protection Several pieces of gear may be placed near each other for added security, if the climber suspects that their placement or the rock quality is not ideal.

Going sideways A traverse is usually protected by several pieces of gear so that the second climber doesn't have to run the risk of a large, swinging fall across the face of the rock.

PORTALEDGE

Home away from home On multi-day, multi-pitch expeditions, climbers may need to bivouac overnight on the rock face, hanging hundreds of feet off the ground. Modern portaledges are collapsible, light, and can fit two climbers and their sleeping bags.

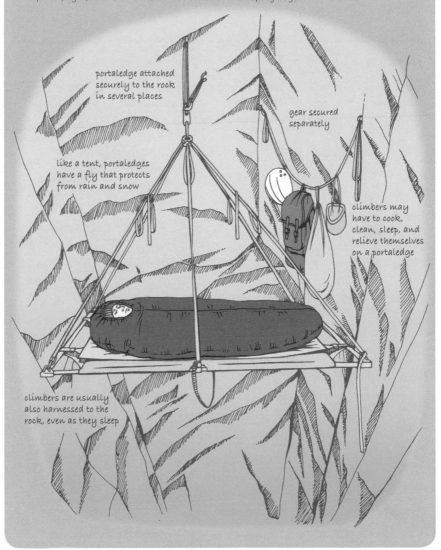

portaledge attached securely to the rock in several places

gear secured separately

like a tent, portaledges have a fly that protects from rain and snow

climbers may have to cook, clean, sleep, and relieve themselves on a portaledge

climbers are usually also harnessed to the rock, even as they sleep

Rappelling

Going down Rather than climbing down, most climbers rappel or "abseil" down a rope, as it is fast and requires very little energy expenditure. Rappellers are not usually belayed by someone else, but control their own speed.

NATURAL ANCHOR POINTS

Bomb proof As a rappeller will place their whole weight and trust in the rope, the anchor to which the rope is secured has to be super secure—or what is popularly termed "bomb proof"—with no chance of slipping or breaking. Immovable boulders and trees are ideal.

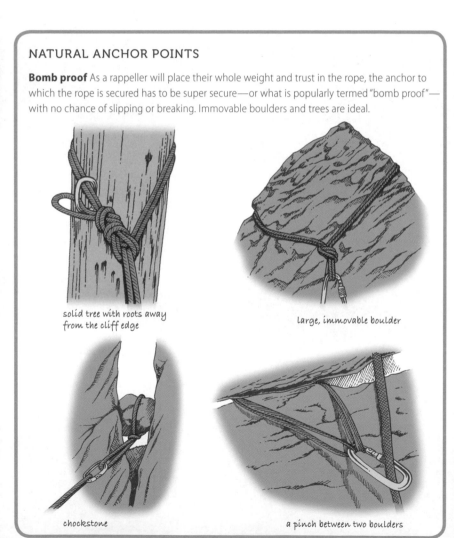

solid tree with roots away
from the cliff edge

large, immovable boulder

chockstone

a pinch between two boulders

Methods Most rappellers now use a descender or the Italian hitch described earlier. However, the original technique, done simply by wrapping the rope around the body to create friction, was developed toward the end of the 19th century.

Classic Using the body as a friction device, the rappeller zigzags the rope through the legs, across the chest, around a shoulder, and across the back to the other arm. They can then walk carefully down the cliff, letting the rope gradually slip through their hands.

Modern Clipping a descender into a harness, a rappeller can make a much safer and more rapid descent, controlling the speed with their lower hand. The top hand should not grip the rope, but just guide it.

Snow and ice climbing

Cold climbing Many of the world's highest peaks are covered in ice and snow, so climbers have long had to contend with the white stuff and its particular dangers. Ice climbing has now become a sport in its own right.

Extreme care
A mountaineer's kit must include protection from the blinding whiteness of the snow and ice, as well as extreme cold and high altitude. Crampons and ice axes are vital.

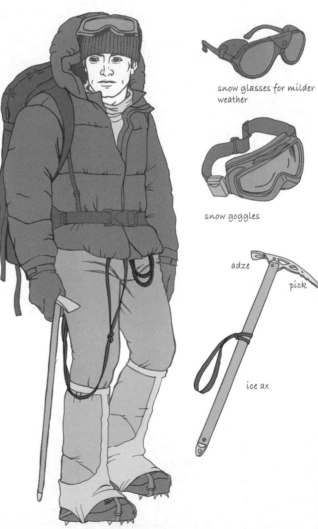

snow glasses for milder weather

snow goggles

adze

pick

ice ax

walking stick/ ski pole

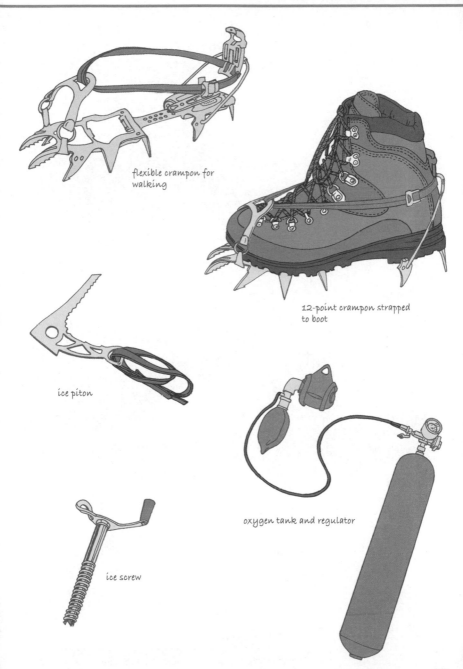

flexible crampon for walking

12-point crampon strapped to boot

ice piton

ice screw

oxygen tank and regulator

183

SELF BELAY

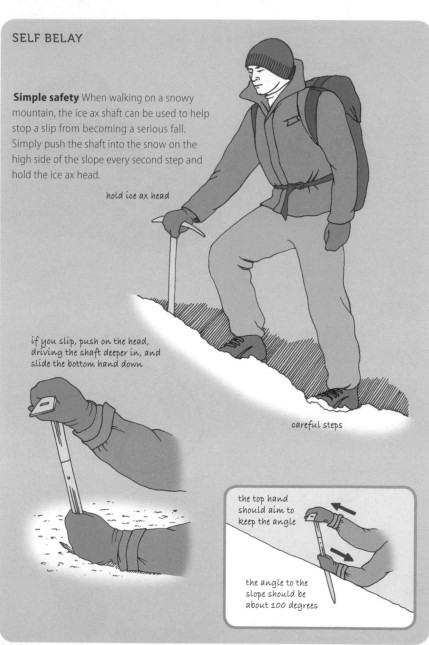

Simple safety When walking on a snowy mountain, the ice ax shaft can be used to help stop a slip from becoming a serious fall. Simply push the shaft into the snow on the high side of the slope every second step and hold the ice ax head.

hold ice ax head

if you slip, push on the head, driving the shaft deeper in, and slide the bottom hand down

careful steps

the top hand should aim to keep the angle

the angle to the slope should be about 100 degrees

SELF-ARREST—HEAD UP, FACE DOWN

Stop the slide If an alpine climber starts sliding, there are several ice-ax techniques that can be used to slow and arrest the fall. These techniques should be well rehearsed before they are needed. Most involve returning to this basic, facedown position.

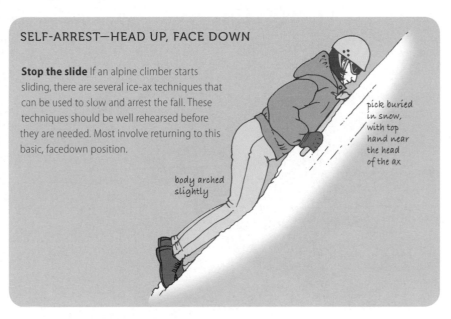

pick buried in snow, with top hand near the head of the ax

body arched slightly

SELF-ARREST—HEAD UP, FACE UP

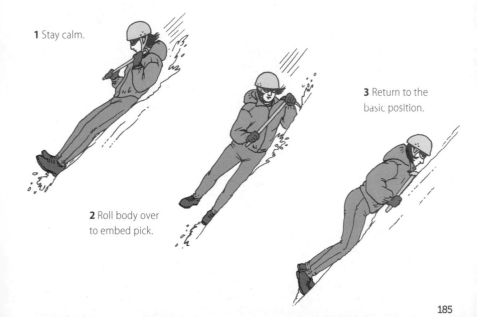

1 Stay calm.

2 Roll body over to embed pick.

3 Return to the basic position.

SELF-ARREST—HEAD DOWN, FACE DOWN

1 Using both hands, aim to put the pick in the snow to the side of your fall trajectory.

2 Keep arms as straight as possible.

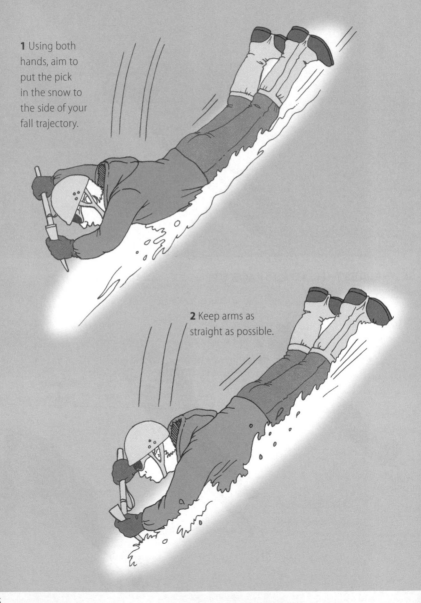

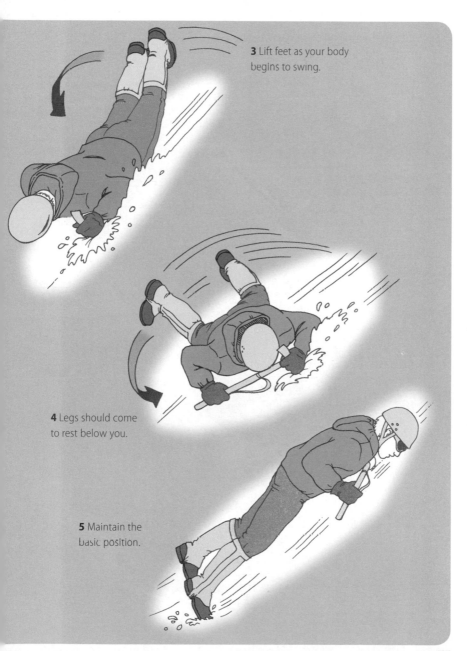

3 Lift feet as your body begins to swing.

4 Legs should come to rest below you.

5 Maintain the basic position.

SELF-ARREST—HEAD DOWN, FACE UP

1 A fall could easily result in being upside down, face up, sliding down the slope.

2 Keep holding the ice ax with both hands.

3 Dig the pick in about hip level.

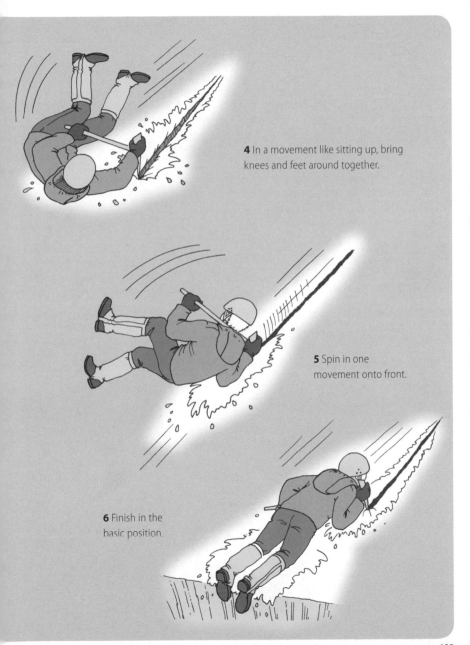

4 In a movement like sitting up, bring knees and feet around together.

5 Spin in one movement onto front.

6 Finish in the basic position.

GLISSADING

Quick way down A fast, controlled descent can be achieved on some slopes by "glissading"—using the ice ax to control speed. This should not be attempted with crampons because they would grip, sending you head over heels.

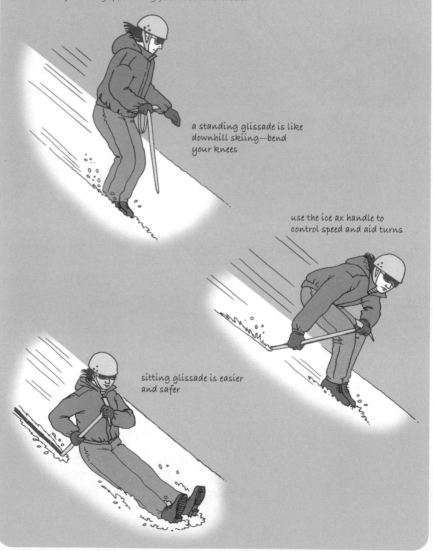

a standing glissade is like downhill skiing—bend your knees

use the ice ax handle to control speed and aid turns

sitting glissade is easier and safer

CUTTING ICE STEPS

Ice stairway Although crampons help, safe descent or ascent on a steep ice slope requires cutting steps. The adze of the ice ax is the best tool.

Descending Using the downhill arm, swing smoothly parallel to your body, chipping a flat surface into the ice. If necessary, the uphill arm can be used for stability.

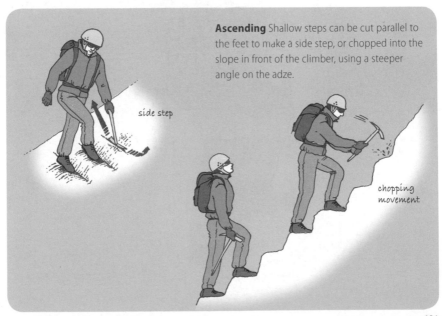

Ascending Shallow steps can be cut parallel to the feet to make a side step, or chopped into the slope in front of the climber, using a steeper angle on the adze.

side step

chopping movement

ICE CLIMBING

Technique With stiff crampons on their feet and an ice ax in each hand, a skilled ice climber can climb frozen waterfalls, walls, or other vertical, solid ice structures. After moving the feet up to a balanced position each time, the lower ax is moved first, then the other one.

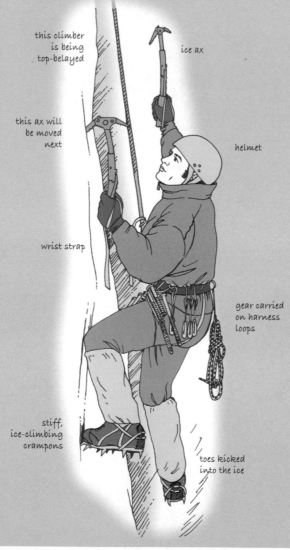

this climber is being top-belayed

ice ax

this ax will be moved next

helmet

wrist strap

gear carried on harness loops

stiff, ice-climbing crampons

toes kicked into the ice

SNOW AND ICE ANCHORS

Cold comfort Like protection in rock climbing, ice screws and other anchors need to be placed carefully to protect against a fall. The quality of the ice where a screw is being placed should be assessed. Modern ice screws need only one hand to put in place.

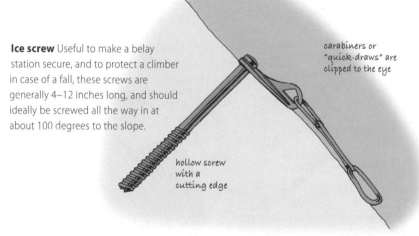

Ice screw Useful to make a belay station secure, and to protect a climber in case of a fall, these screws are generally 4–12 inches long, and should ideally be screwed all the way in at about 100 degrees to the slope.

carabiners or "quick-draws" are clipped to the eye

hollow screw with a cutting edge

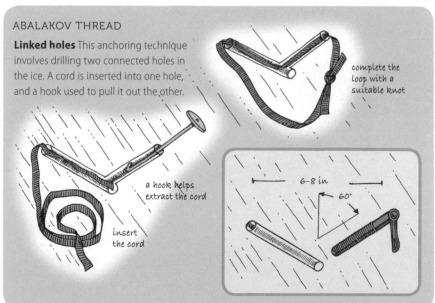

ABALAKOV THREAD

Linked holes This anchoring technique involves drilling two connected holes in the ice. A cord is inserted into one hole, and a hook used to pull it out the other.

complete the loop with a suitable knot

a hook helps extract the cord

insert the cord

6–8 in

60°

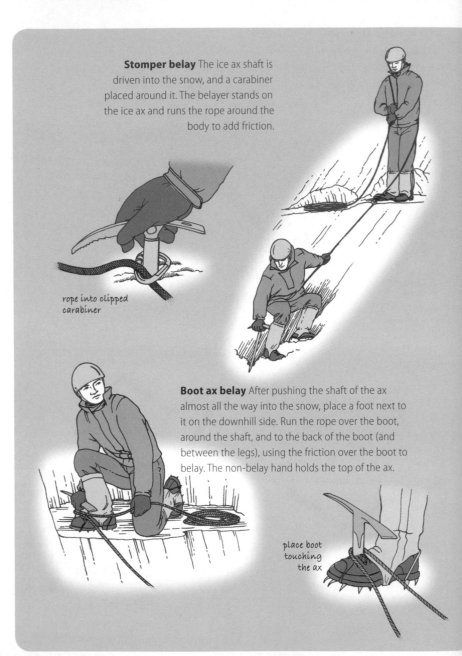

Stomper belay The ice ax shaft is driven into the snow, and a carabiner placed around it. The belayer stands on the ice ax and runs the rope around the body to add friction.

rope into clipped carabiner

Boot ax belay After pushing the shaft of the ax almost all the way into the snow, place a foot next to it on the downhill side. Run the rope over the boot, around the shaft, and to the back of the boot (and between the legs), using the friction over the boot to belay. The non-belay hand holds the top of the ax.

place boot touching the ax

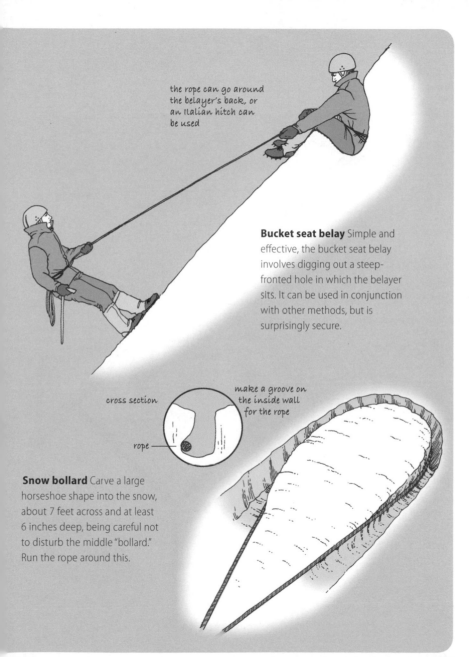

the rope can go around the belayer's back, or an Italian hitch can be used

Bucket seat belay Simple and effective, the bucket seat belay involves digging out a steep-fronted hole in which the belayer sits. It can be used in conjunction with other methods, but is surprisingly secure.

cross section

make a groove on the inside wall for the rope

rope

Snow bollard Carve a large horseshoe shape into the snow, about 7 feet across and at least 6 inches deep, being careful not to disturb the middle "bollard." Run the rope around this.

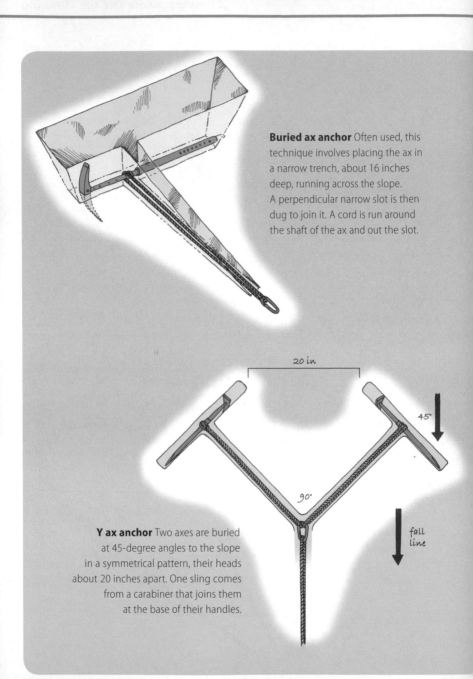

Buried ax anchor Often used, this technique involves placing the ax in a narrow trench, about 16 inches deep, running across the slope. A perpendicular narrow slot is then dug to join it. A cord is run around the shaft of the ax and out the slot.

20 in

45°

90°

fall line

Y ax anchor Two axes are buried at 45-degree angles to the slope in a symmetrical pattern, their heads about 20 inches apart. One sling comes from a carabiner that joins them at the base of their handles.

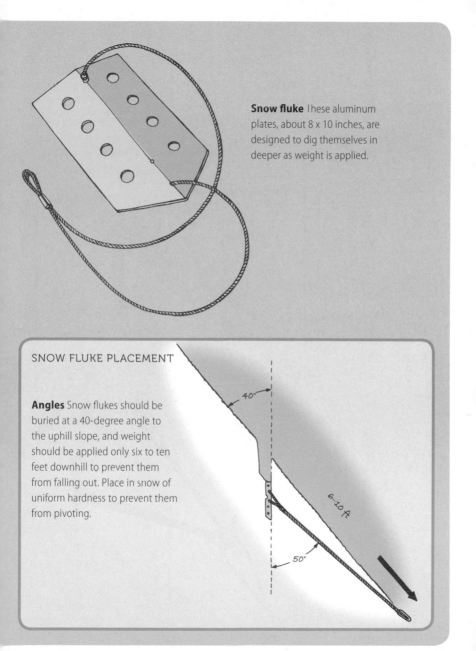

Snow fluke These aluminum plates, about 8 x 10 inches, are designed to dig themselves in deeper as weight is applied.

SNOW FLUKE PLACEMENT

Angles Snow flukes should be buried at a 40-degree angle to the uphill slope, and weight should be applied only six to ten feet downhill to prevent them from falling out. Place in snow of uniform hardness to prevent them from pivoting.

40°

6–10 ft

50°

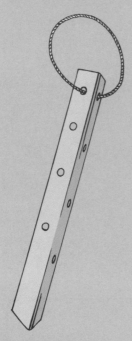

Picket Pickets are usually about 2 feet long and made of aluminum. They need to be well driven into hard-packed snow or ice.

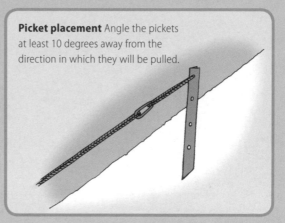

Picket placement Angle the pickets at least 10 degrees away from the direction in which they will be pulled.

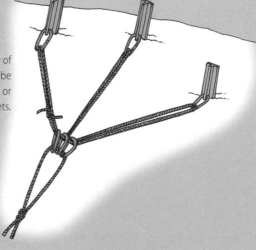

3 pickets To increase the security of a picket anchor, the load can be evenly distributed over three or more pickets.

Avalanche awareness

Great white killer Quickly reaching speeds of up to 80 mph and wiping out everything in their path, avalanches are a serious hazard in steep areas with lots of snow. About 150 people are killed in avalanches each year.

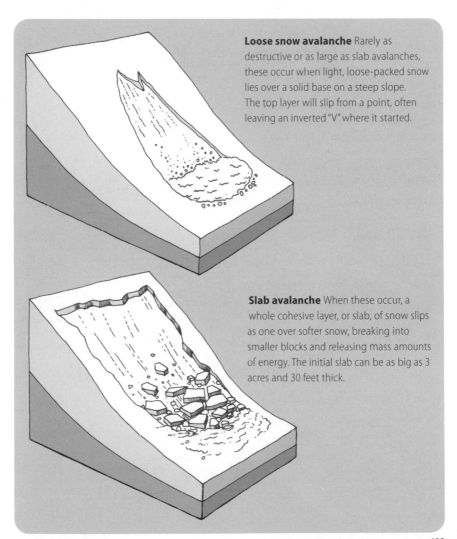

Loose snow avalanche Rarely as destructive or as large as slab avalanches, these occur when light, loose-packed snow lies over a solid base on a steep slope. The top layer will slip from a point, often leaving an inverted "V" where it started.

Slab avalanche When these occur, a whole cohesive layer, or slab, of snow slips as one over softer snow, breaking into smaller blocks and releasing mass amounts of energy. The initial slab can be as big as 3 acres and 30 feet thick.

SNOWPACK LAYERS

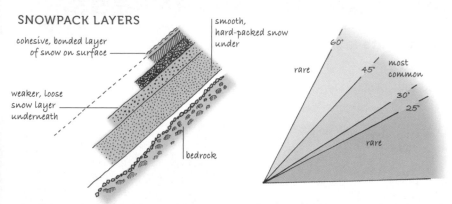

cohesive, bonded layer of snow on surface

smooth, hard-packed snow under

weaker, loose snow layer underneath

bedrock

60°

rare

45°

most common

30°

25°

rare

Consistency A cohesive slab over a loose layer, which in turn sits on a hard-packed smooth surface, is ideal for a slab avalanche.

Steepness Slabs occur mostly on slopes of 30–45 degrees. Steeper slopes naturally have more frequent, small, soft-snow avalanches.

DANGEROUS PLACES

What lies beneath Beware of steep places where snow accumulates, such as cornices, convex slopes, and the lee side of ridges.

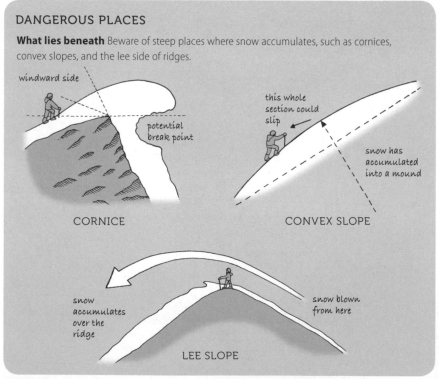

windward side

potential break point

CORNICE

this whole section could slip

snow has accumulated into a mound

CONVEX SLOPE

snow accumulates over the ridge

snow blown from here

LEE SLOPE

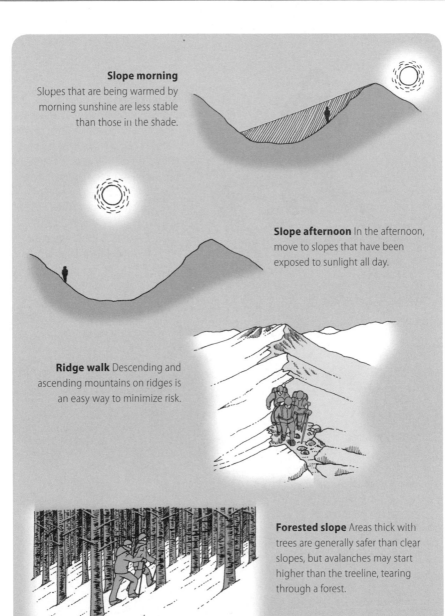

Slope morning Slopes that are being warmed by morning sunshine are less stable than those in the shade.

Slope afternoon In the afternoon, move to slopes that have been exposed to sunlight all day.

Ridge walk Descending and ascending mountains on ridges is an easy way to minimize risk.

Forested slope Areas thick with trees are generally safer than clear slopes, but avalanches may start higher than the treeline, tearing through a forest.

RUTSCHBLOCK TEST

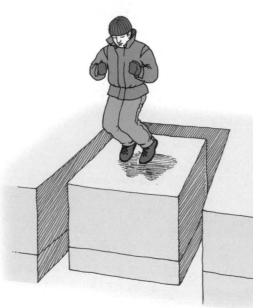

Stability test On a slope of 30 degrees or more, carve out a large block on all sides, about 5 feet deep. It should be big enough to stand or ski on. Have someone watch the front face as you carefully stand, then lightly jump, and then fully jump on it. If fractures appear with light pressure or movement, the slope is unstable, but if no fractures appear after much movement, it is stable.

SHOVEL SHEAR TEST

Identify weakness Cut or dig down into the snow until you reach a hard layer (no more than two feet down, and usually just a shovel blade). Dig or cut out three sides of a straight-sided small block, about one foot across. Place the shovel blade behind the block and pull it forward. The block will "shear" off on weak layers, and the ease with which it does so will reveal much about the quality of the snowpack.

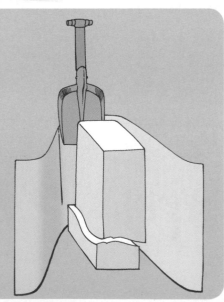

AVALANCHE RESCUE

Life savers In the event someone is caught in an avalanche, quick rescue is vital for their survival. Modern equipment, such as beacons, can dramatically increase the chance of survival.

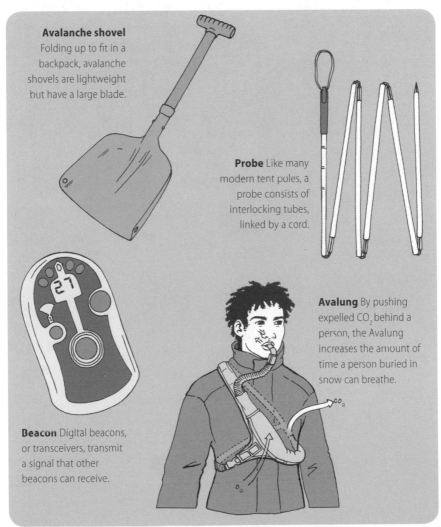

Avalanche shovel
Folding up to fit in a backpack, avalanche shovels are lightweight but have a large blade.

Probe Like many modern tent poles, a probe consists of interlocking tubes, linked by a cord.

Avalung By pushing expelled CO_2 behind a person, the Avalung increases the amount of time a person buried in snow can breathe.

Beacon Digital beacons, or transceivers, transmit a signal that other beacons can receive.

AIRBAG

Back-up plan An avalanche airbag is worn like a backpack, but, if triggered, inflates large air cavities, which gives the person caught in an avalanche more chance of staying on top of the avalanche and being found quickly.

pack weighs about 7 pounds

inflates as much as 6 cubic feet of air

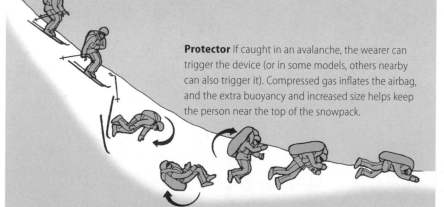

Protector If caught in an avalanche, the wearer can trigger the device (or in some models, others nearby can also trigger it). Compressed gas inflates the airbag, and the extra buoyancy and increased size helps keep the person near the top of the snowpack.

SEARCH AREA

Likely spots On a steep slope with no deviations, make an imaginary line following the last sightings of the person. Their tracks may help. The search area should be where the slope flattens out. It is vital to find someone quickly—research has shown that survival chances of buried skiers drop to just 30 percent after 35 minutes, and to 0 after 2 hours.

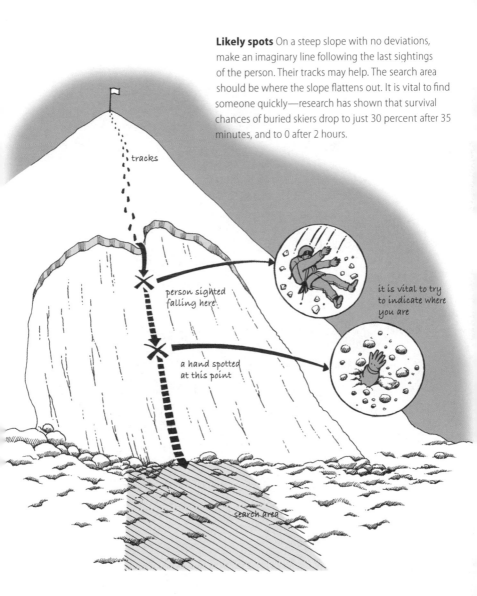

tracks

person sighted falling here

it is vital to try to indicate where you are

a hand spotted at this point

search area

Gully The natural flow down a winding gully means a person could be at any of the wide corners, where the snow decelerates.

Bench Because of the middle flat section, a person who fell in the top of this avalanche could be half-way up, or down the bottom.

PROBE LINE

Search party Standing about 2.5 feet apart, searchers probe down to the bottom of the soft snow, up to 10 feet deep. They then step forward 2 feet and repeat.

BEACON SEARCH

Beep test Modern avalanche beacons all operate on a frequency of 457 kHz, so are compatible. Rescuers turn their beacons to "receive." Then, they spread out and search in fixed patterns, narrowing down the search once a signal is received.

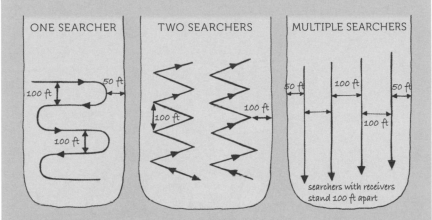

CLOSING IN

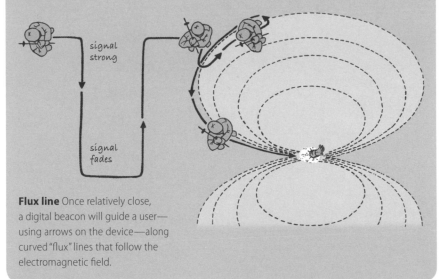

Flux line Once relatively close, a digital beacon will guide a user—using arrows on the device—along curved "flux" lines that follow the electromagnetic field.

MOUNTAIN BIKING

The relatively new sport of mountain biking is all about freedom and adventure. With a bike, you can get deep into the wild, push yourself to your limits, and enjoy the thrill of a downhill run—all in one day.

KNOW YOUR MOUNTAIN BIKE

Freedom machine Mountain bikes are built for safe and comfortable travel on rough and steep terrain. They have low-slung, robust frames, large tires, lots of gears, and powerful brakes.

Cycle choice Mountain bikes may look similar to each other at first glance, but there is a wide variation in frame materials, design, suspension, fittings, and, of course, price. Beware of cheap bikes masquerading as mountain bikes—they won't last long.

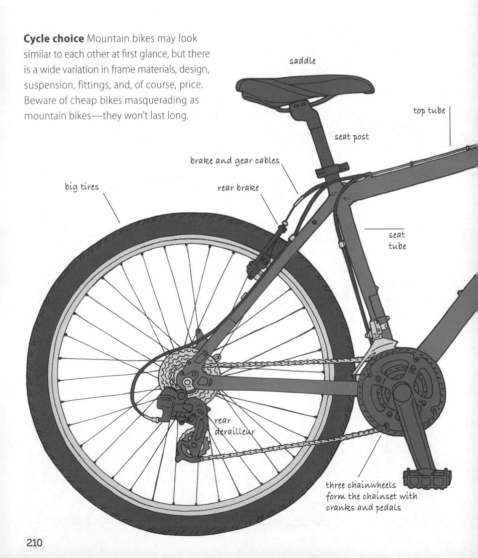

saddle

top tube

seat post

brake and gear cables

rear brake

big tires

seat tube

rear derailleur

three chainwheels form the chainset with cranks and pedals

rear brake lever

front brake lever

gear shifter
(front derailleur)

gear shifter
(rear derailleur)

handlebar

stem

Handlebar Mountain bike handlebars are
straight and wide. The gear shifters are usually
on the underside, but may be above. Grip
shifters are mounted around the handlebars.

front brake
cable

front brake

front fork

down
tube

TRANSMISSION

Power to the wheel The transmission system transmits power from the pedals to the rear wheel via a chain. Some bicycles have a fixed single gear arrangement, which is light and mechanically simple, but if you want to climb every mountain and nail every descent, you will need a wide range of gears and the technology to swiftly change from one to another. Mountain bikes have two gear shifters: one to move the chain on the three forward chainrings and one to move it onto the (usually seven) rear sprockets. A derailleur at each end of the transmission does the job of shifting the chain.

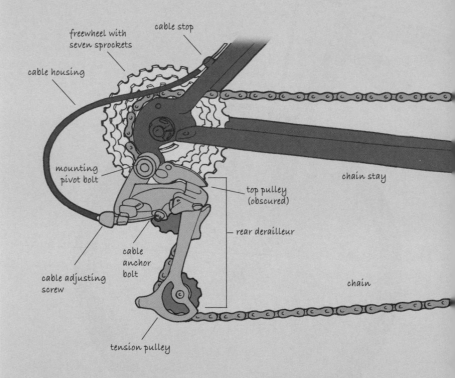

freewheel with
seven sprockets

cable stop

cable housing

mounting
pivot bolt

top pulley
(obscured)

chain stay

rear derailleur

cable
anchor
bolt

cable adjusting
screw

chain

tension pulley

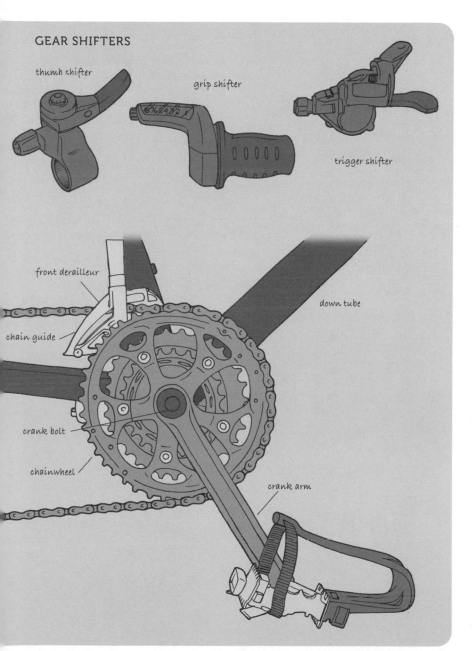

GEAR SHIFTERS

thumb shifter

grip shifter

trigger shifter

front derailleur

down tube

chain guide

crank bolt

chainwheel

crank arm

BRAKES

Stopping power When you're zooming down a mountain pass at high speed, it's good to know that you have powerful, reliable, and responsive brakes at your fingertips.

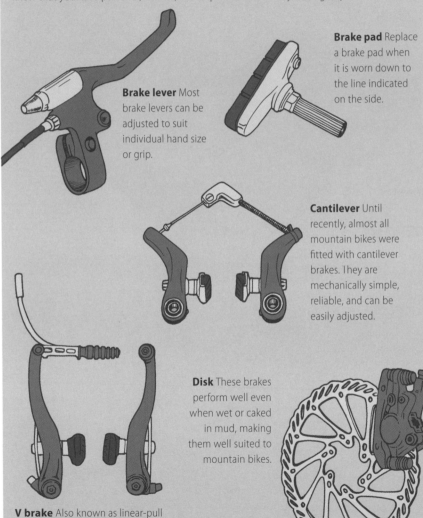

Brake lever Most brake levers can be adjusted to suit individual hand size or grip.

Brake pad Replace a brake pad when it is worn down to the line indicated on the side.

Cantilever Until recently, almost all mountain bikes were fitted with cantilever brakes. They are mechanically simple, reliable, and can be easily adjusted.

Disk These brakes perform well even when wet or caked in mud, making them well suited to mountain bikes.

V brake Also known as linear-pull brakes, V brakes are powerful and very simple to maintain.

PEDALS

Where foot meets machine Pedals are your primary means for controlling your bike. The pedals you get can make a big difference in how you ride and how your bike performs.

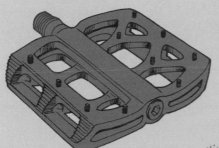

Platform These pedals provide a wide, stable surface to support your feet. They are the easiest pedals to disengage from in the event of a crash and are recommended for beginners.

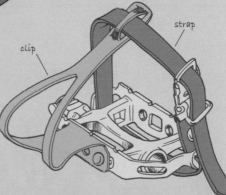

clip

strap

Clip and strap By adding a toeclip and strap to a platform pedal design, you can greatly increase your efficiency throughout the pedal stroke.

Clipless When connected to a matching cycling shoe, clipless pedals put you totally at one with your bike with no loss of efficiency.

Cleated shoe Cycling shoes range from summer sandals to winter boots. Ensure that your choice is compatible with the clipless system on your bike.

Narrow saddle These saddles allow you to easily slide off the back when descending.

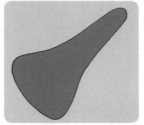

Wide saddle A wider saddle may be appropriate if you're taking longer trips.

Women's saddle Women have wider hips than men and may benefit from a wide saddle.

FULL SUSPENSION BIKE

Nice ride For a little extra cost and weight, a full suspension bike will give you lots more comfort, enjoyment, and control.

rear suspension

front suspension fork

damping adjustment

oil reservoir

Rear shock absorber
A spring and damping mechanism work in unison.

spring

Front fork Telescopic front forks can be tuned to suit particular riding conditions.

SINGLE PIVOT

Simple suspension A single pivot design is the simplest type of rear suspension. It consists of a shock absorber and a simple swingarm that connects the rear axle to a single pivot point.

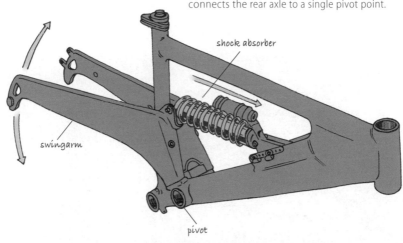

shock absorber

swingarm

pivot

FOUR BAR

Smooth rider This design uses several linkage points to activate the shock absorber. These linkages allow the rear axle to move in an almost vertical path for superior performance.

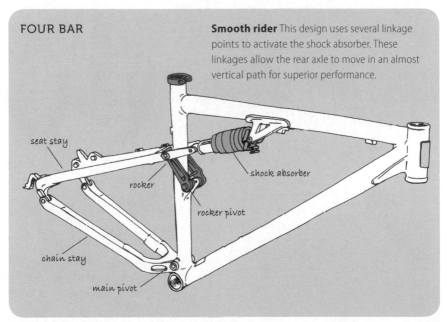

seat stay

rocker

shock absorber

rocker pivot

chain stay

main pivot

Accessories

Extras A bike alone will only get you so far. You'll need a few extras to keep it running smoothly and safely, and with a little extra expenditure you can give it some luggage capacity and keep it safe from thieves.

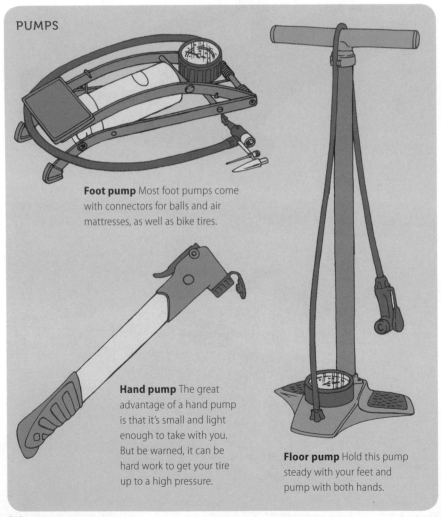

PUMPS

Foot pump Most foot pumps come with connectors for balls and air mattresses, as well as bike tires.

Hand pump The great advantage of a hand pump is that it's small and light enough to take with you. But be warned, it can be hard work to get your tire up to a high pressure.

Floor pump Hold this pump steady with your feet and pump with both hands.

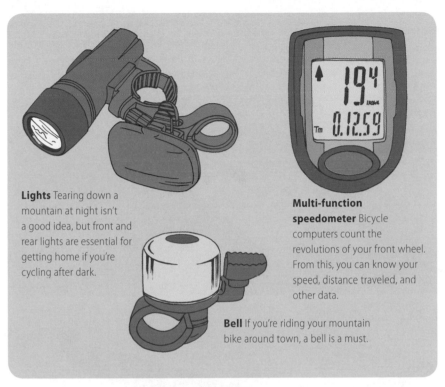

Lights Tearing down a mountain at night isn't a good idea, but front and rear lights are essential for getting home if you're cycling after dark.

Multi-function speedometer Bicycle computers count the revolutions of your front wheel. From this, you can know your speed, distance traveled, and other data.

Bell If you're riding your mountain bike around town, a bell is a must.

LOCKS

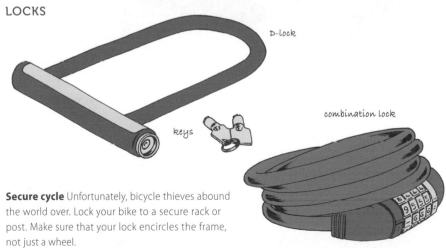

D-lock

keys

combination lock

Secure cycle Unfortunately, bicycle thieves abound the world over. Lock your bike to a secure rack or post. Make sure that your lock encircles the frame, not just a wheel.

PUNCTURE REPAIR KIT

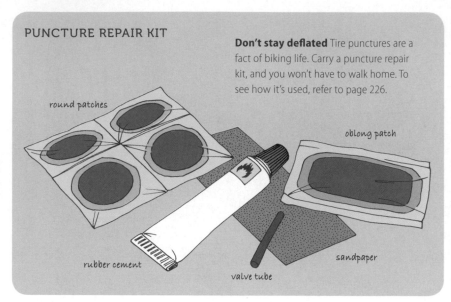

Don't stay deflated Tire punctures are a fact of biking life. Carry a puncture repair kit, and you won't have to walk home. To see how it's used, refer to page 226.

round patches

oblong patch

rubber cement

valve tube

sandpaper

TOOLS

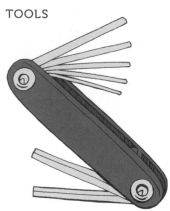

Tire lever Use the spoon end to pry the tire off the rim. The hook goes around a spoke to hold it in place.

Allen key set Pretty much anything that's bolted on to a modern mountain bike can be loosened and reattached with an appropriately sized allen key.

Chain tool Use this tool to repair a broken or damaged chain. To see how it works, refer to page 224.

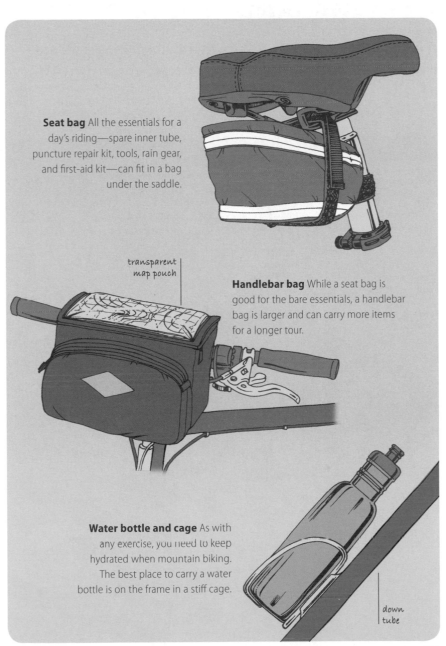

Seat bag All the essentials for a day's riding—spare inner tube, puncture repair kit, tools, rain gear, and first-aid kit—can fit in a bag under the saddle.

transparent
map pouch

Handlebar bag While a seat bag is good for the bare essentials, a handlebar bag is larger and can carry more items for a longer tour.

Water bottle and cage As with any exercise, you need to keep hydrated when mountain biking. The best place to carry a water bottle is on the frame in a stiff cage.

down
tube

Fitting and Adjustment

A bike made for you When you ride a bike that's the right size and properly set up, you will feel comfortable and confident, and you will be riding with maximum efficiency.

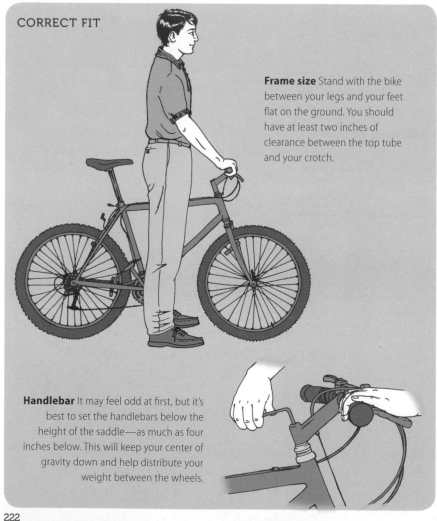

CORRECT FIT

Frame size Stand with the bike between your legs and your feet flat on the ground. You should have at least two inches of clearance between the top tube and your crotch.

Handlebar It may feel odd at first, but it's best to set the handlebars below the height of the saddle—as much as four inches below. This will keep your center of gravity down and help distribute your weight between the wheels.

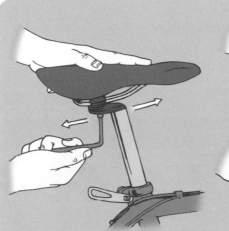

Saddle fore–aft position Rotate the pedals until one foot is at the three o'clock position. With a properly positioned saddle, the indentation just below your knee cap will be directly above the axle of the pedal.

Saddle height Put your pedal in line with your seat tube and at the bottom of its stroke. Set the saddle to the height where your heel can just touch the pedal with a straight leg.

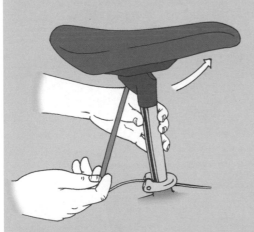

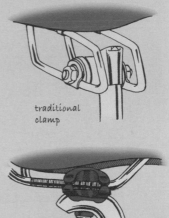

traditional clamp

microclamp

Saddle tilt Start with the seat level to the ground. If you experience discomfort, angle the seat up or down by no more than about three degrees.

Running repairs

Quick fixes Broken chains, punctures, and buckled wheels can quickly bring you to a halt. But with a few tools and a bit of know-how, you can be back in the saddle.

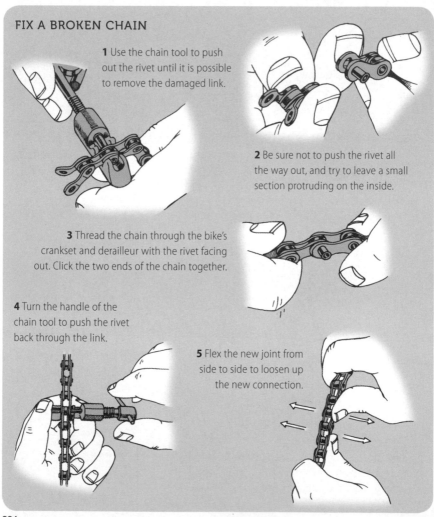

FIX A BROKEN CHAIN

1 Use the chain tool to push out the rivet until it is possible to remove the damaged link.

2 Be sure not to push the rivet all the way out, and try to leave a small section protruding on the inside.

3 Thread the chain through the bike's crankset and derailleur with the rivet facing out. Click the two ends of the chain together.

4 Turn the handle of the chain tool to push the rivet back through the link.

5 Flex the new joint from side to side to loosen up the new connection.

REPLACE A TUBE

1 Release your brakes and remove the wheel from the bike.

2 Grab the tire with both hands and roll it to unseat the bead from the rim.

3 Use a tire lever to pry the tire off the wheel all the way around.

4 Slightly inflate the new or repaired inner tube and tuck it back into the tire.

5 Push the tire bead back over the rim wall, using your thumbs and fingers.

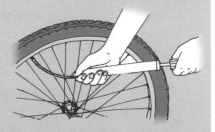

6 Pump up the tire, checking that it is seated properly.

FIX A PUNCTURE

1 Find the hole by inflating the tube and running it past your lips. Alternatively, put it underwater and look for bubbles.

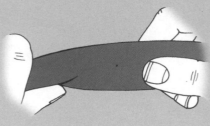

2 Examine the puncture so you know exactly where to place the patch. Mark the site in some way so you don't lose it.

3 Use sandpaper to roughen the area around the puncture. This will give the adhesive a good surface to grip onto.

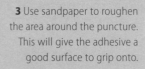

4 Place a small amount of adhesive around the hole. Spread it with your fingers over an area slightly larger than the patch you are going to apply.

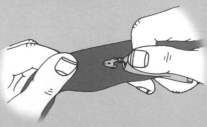

5 When the adhesive is dry to the touch, separate the patch from its protective film and press it firmly down on the hole.

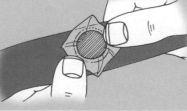

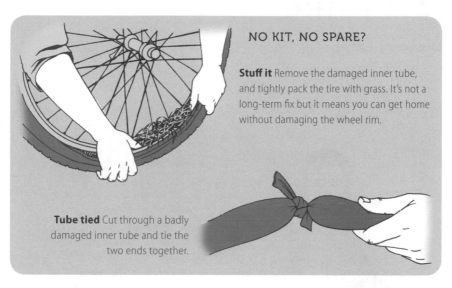

NO KIT, NO SPARE?

Stuff it Remove the damaged inner tube, and tightly pack the tire with grass. It's not a long-term fix but it means you can get home without damaging the wheel rim.

Tube tied Cut through a badly damaged inner tube and tie the two ends together.

BUCKLED WHEEL

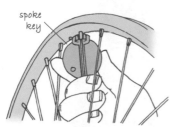

spoke key

Final check Spin the wheel in your hands and look out for any remaining wobbles that need fixing.

Twist fix A slightly warped wheel can be fixed by adjusting the tension on the spokes.

Step on it A badly buckled wheel might require some brute force.

CLOTHING

Dressing for adventure No matter what type of mountain biking trip you have in mind—and whatever the weather—your clothing should be geared toward your safety and comfort.

All the gear You don't have to wear the latest high tech cycling gear to ride a mountain bike, but it helps. Specially designed cycling clothing helps to keep you at a comfortable temperature, whether you're climbing a hill or freewheeling down the other side.

lightweight cycling shirt

gloves

lycra shorts

lightweight waterproof shoes

elasticized pocket

Helmet Protecting your head when riding a trail is an absolute must. Ensure that your helmet conforms to standards and is the right fit.

side view

front view

straps should fit snugly under the chin

Glasses Good quality glasses will keep ultraviolet light, wind, dust, and bugs out of your eyes.

full-finger

fingerless

Jacket Pack a lightweight wind- and waterproof jacket.

Gloves Padded gloves are a good idea for long rides, and will protect your hands if you fall off.

RIDING TECHNIQUE

Trail skills Take your mountain bike off road and you'll need to develop some new riding skills suited to rough terrain. It's all part of the fun, and once you learn to ride a mountain bike, you never forget!

The riding position A comfortable and efficient riding position will get you feeling relaxed, and will enable you to ride longer distances with less effort.

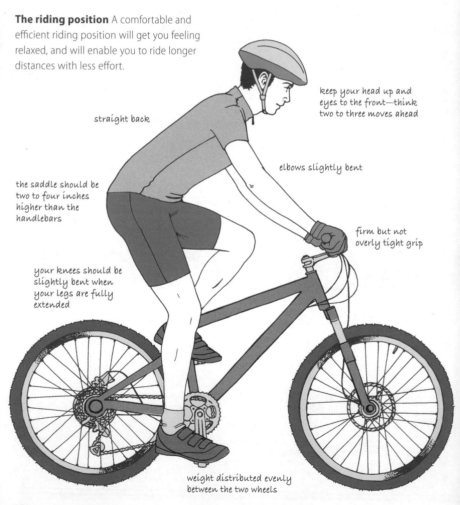

keep your head up and eyes to the front—think two to three moves ahead

straight back

elbows slightly bent

the saddle should be two to four inches higher than the handlebars

firm but not overly tight grip

your knees should be slightly bent when your legs are fully extended

weight distributed evenly between the two wheels

MOUNTING

1 Stand on the left side of the bike, away from the chain. Hold the handlebars with both hands. The right pedal should be in the two o'clock position.

2 Lift your right leg over the back of the saddle, and place your right foot on the pedal.

3 Flick the pedal around to engage the toe-clip or cleat mechanism. Push off with your left foot. As the left pedal comes around to the top, place your left foot on the pedal and continue pedaling.

RUNNING DISMOUNT

1 Use the brakes to slow the bike to a running or walking pace. Unclip your right leg and swing it over the back wheel.

2 While the bike is still in motion, bring your right foot in front of your left foot and step down onto the ground.

3 Grab the bike by the top tube, haul it over your shoulder, and walk or run past the obstacle.

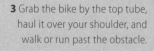

Ascend Shift down to a lower gear before a hill gets really steep. Slide forward in the saddle to put more weight on the front wheel. Bend your elbows and hunch down a little.

pump your back brakes to control your speed going downhill

Descend On steep descents keep your weight toward the back of the bike to stop the bike from toppling forward. Look ahead and pick your line.

233

LOG HOP

1 Reduce speed as you approach the log, and change down to a low gear. Approach the log at 90 degrees.

2 Compress your body by bending your arms and pushing down toward your handlebars. Then, jerk your body upright and pull up on your handlebars.

3 As the front wheel clears the log, shift your body weight forward to minimize load on the rear wheel.

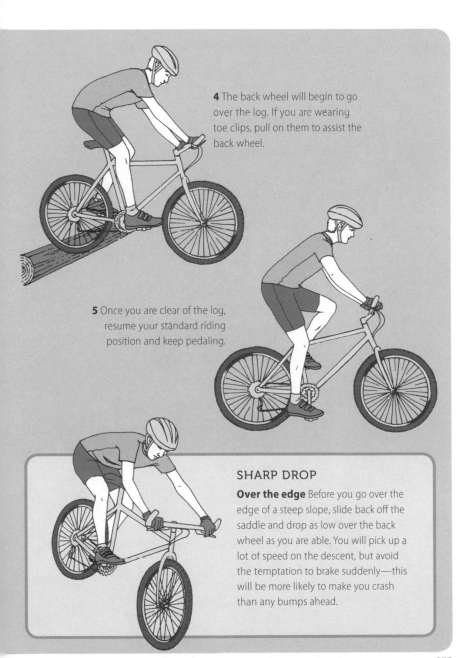

4 The back wheel will begin to go over the log. If you are wearing toe clips, pull on them to assist the back wheel.

5 Once you are clear of the log, resume your standard riding position and keep pedaling.

SHARP DROP

Over the edge Before you go over the edge of a steep slope, slide back off the saddle and drop as low over the back wheel as you are able. You will pick up a lot of speed on the descent, but avoid the temptation to brake suddenly—this will be more likely to make you crash than any bumps ahead.

CORNERING

1 Brake to a safe speed before you enter a corner. Look as far ahead as possible and pick the best line to take.

2 Lean your bike into the bend while keeping your body upright. On extreme corners, you may want to drop your inside foot to place on the ground if you start to slide.

3 As you complete the bend, check your exit line. Bring your weight forward and start pedaling as soon as you can.

High-speed cornering
Take the widest possible line when entering the corner. Keep your outside leg extended as this will help you to maintain traction. Lean into the corner and do not brake as this is the most likely thing to make you lose control.

STEP HOPPING

1 Approach the step straight on while riding slowly. Lean back and try to balance all your body weight over the rear wheel.

2 Pull up on the handlebars when you are about eight inches from the step. This will lift your front wheel over the top.

3 Lean forward and dab your front brake. This will cause the rear wheel to lift up.

4 Release the brake, shift your weight back, and resume normal riding.

BUNNY HOP

1 Load yourself like a spring by crouching on the bike with bent elbows, knees, and hips. Go easy on the speed, and level your cranks.

2 From the crouch, spring your body upward while pulling on the handlebars.

3 As the front wheel reaches full height, throw the handlebars forward. Lift your legs and feet to raise the rear wheel.

4 Land on both wheels simultaneously, or, if that is not possible, the back tire first. Absorb the impact with your slightly bent arms and legs.

CROSSING WATER

1 If you can't see the bottom of an unfamiliar watercourse, stop and investigate. If it looks passable, approach in a low gear.

2 Pedal fast as your front wheel enters the water.

3 Continue pedaling the whole way through. If you stop, you'll come to a quick halt and may fall in.

4 As you exit the water, pedal faster to get out of the river and up the opposite bank.

WASH AND LUBRICATE

Shiny again Good mountain biking is a filthy business. A well-made bike can work fine when caked in mud and grit, but for the sake of your machine and your safety, give it a good wash and service when you get home.

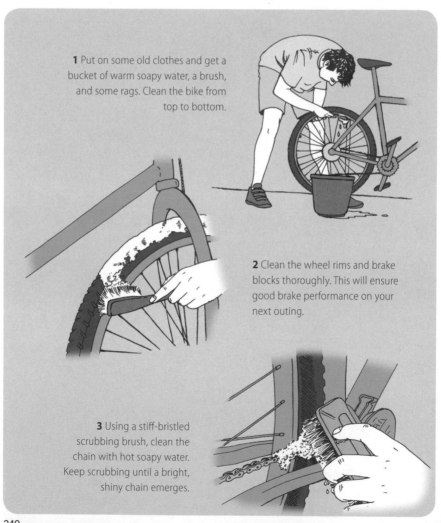

1 Put on some old clothes and get a bucket of warm soapy water, a brush, and some rags. Clean the bike from top to bottom.

2 Clean the wheel rims and brake blocks thoroughly. This will ensure good brake performance on your next outing.

3 Using a stiff-bristled scrubbing brush, clean the chain with hot soapy water. Keep scrubbing until a bright, shiny chain emerges.

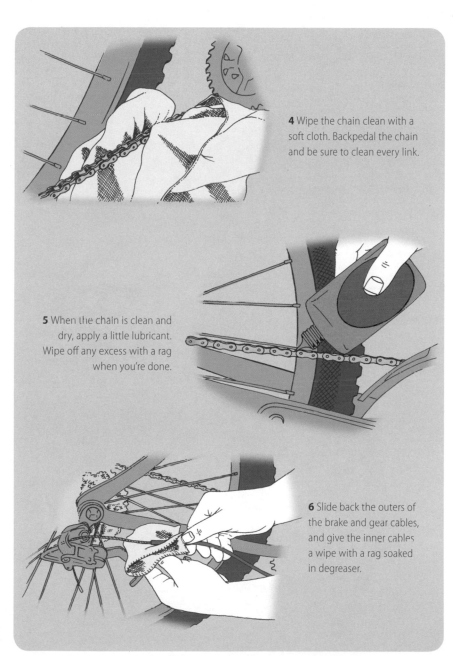

4 Wipe the chain clean with a soft cloth. Backpedal the chain and be sure to clean every link.

5 When the chain is clean and dry, apply a little lubricant. Wipe off any excess with a rag when you're done.

6 Slide back the outers of the brake and gear cables, and give the inner cables a wipe with a rag soaked in degreaser.

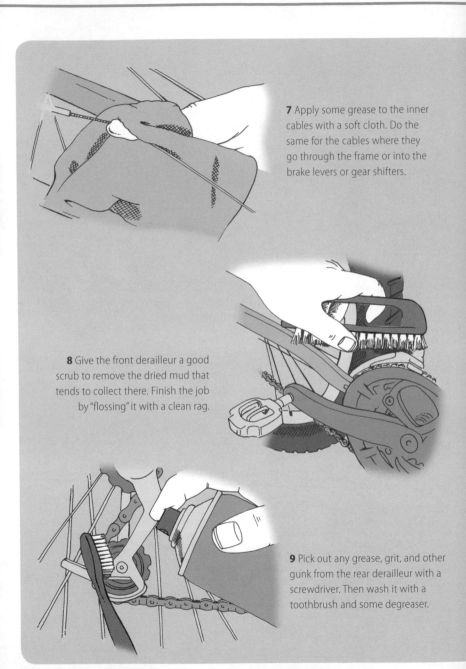

7 Apply some grease to the inner cables with a soft cloth. Do the same for the cables where they go through the frame or into the brake levers or gear shifters.

8 Give the front derailleur a good scrub to remove the dried mud that tends to collect there. Finish the job by "flossing" it with a clean rag.

9 Pick out any grease, grit, and other gunk from the rear derailleur with a screwdriver. Then wash it with a toothbrush and some degreaser.

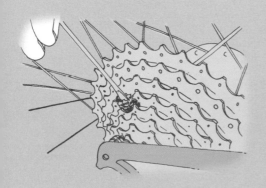

10 Pick through the space between the rear sprockets with a screwdriver to remove any large clumps of grease and mud.

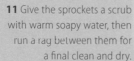

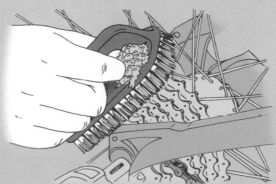

11 Give the sprockets a scrub with warm soapy water, then run a rag between them for a final clean and dry.

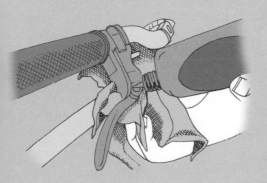

12 To finish, apply a few drops of lubricant to the brake lever and gear shifter pivots.

CANOEING AND KAYAKING

Our planet is two-thirds water. If you like to get outdoors and into nature, you are missing out if you're not in a boat. Canoes and kayaks offer the adventurer vast new horizons to explore.

Know your boat

Freedom afloat Canoes and kayaks are human-powered boats. They are small and light enough to be easily propelled and steered by one or two people, but can still be packed for an extended expedition.

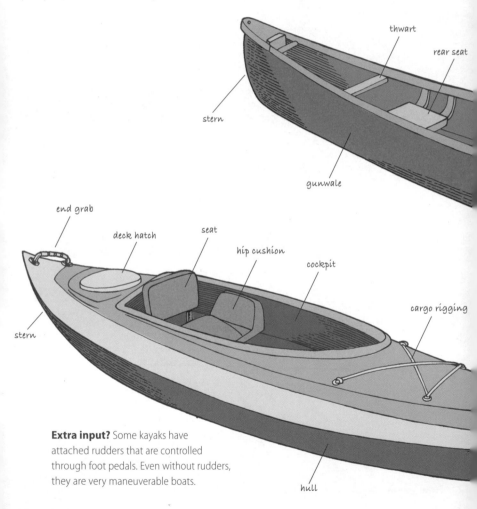

thwart

rear seat

stern

gunwale

end grab

deck hatch

seat

hip cushion

cockpit

cargo rigging

stern

Extra input? Some kayaks have attached rudders that are controlled through foot pedals. Even without rudders, they are very maneuverable boats.

hull

Canoe The canoe is the original (and many say the best) way to take to the water. Canoes are small, narrow boats that are usually propelled and steered using single-bladed paddles, but they may also be poled, rowed, or sailed. They may even be picked up and carried from one watercourse to another. Canoes are usually most efficient with two paddlers on board.

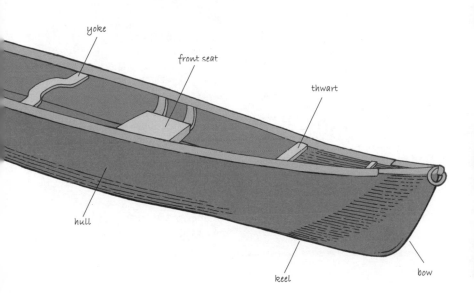

yoke

front seat

thwart

hull

keel

bow

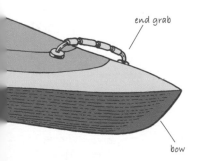

end grab

bow

Kayak Modern kayaks take the same basic form as the wood, whalebone, and sealskin hunting boats developed by the Inuit people thousands of years ago. Kayaks usually have a covered deck with one or two cockpits that may be enclosed with a spray skirt. Kayaks are propelled using a double blade paddle.

HULLS

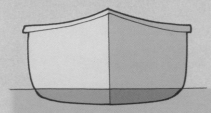

Flat Highly stable on calm water. Easily steered. Good choice for anglers and recreational paddlers.

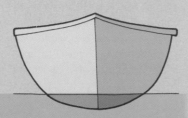

Round These hulls are designed for speed and efficiency. They can feel unstable, but are actually very resistant to capsizing.

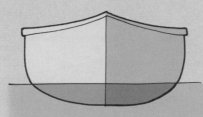

Shallow arch These provide a compromise between flat and round hulls.

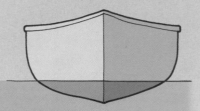

Shallow V A reasonably stable design with good tracking and maneuverability.

STEM

Rounded A rounded stem aids steering and maneuverability and is a good choice for paddling in moving water.

Squared A square stem will help the track or straight-line performance of a canoe. It is suited to flat water or touring.

KEEL

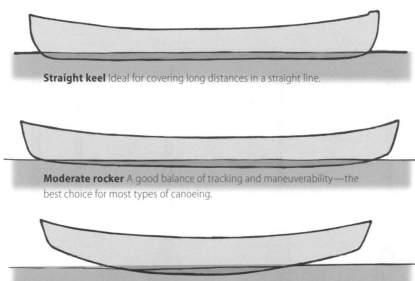

Straight keel Ideal for covering long distances in a straight line.

Moderate rocker A good balance of tracking and maneuverability—the best choice for most types of canoeing.

Highly rockered Excellent maneuverability—good for whitewater canoeing in extreme conditions.

SYMMETRY

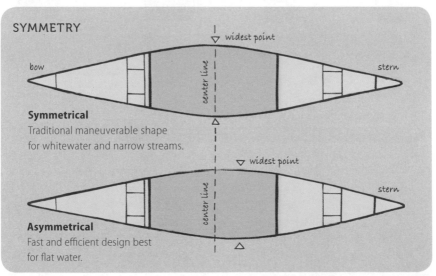

widest point

bow

center line

stern

Symmetrical
Traditional maneuverable shape
for whitewater and narrow streams.

widest point

center line

stern

Asymmetrical
Fast and efficient design best
for flat water.

Paddles

Means of propulsion The type of paddle you choose will depend on your physique, boat type, and intended use. Paddles are crafted from fiberglass, aluminum, carbon fiber, plastic, or traditional wood.

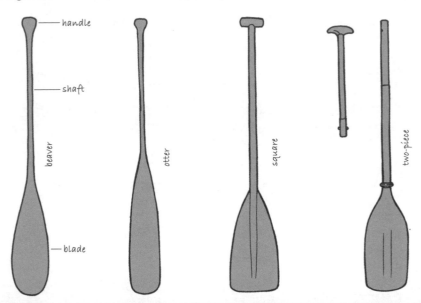

handle

shaft

beaver

blade

otter

square

two-piece

CANOES AND KAYAKS THROUGH HISTORY

Algonquin 1–6 persons; birch and wood; everyday transport, hunting, and fishing.

Inuit 1 person; seal skins and whale bones; hunting and fishing.

Umiak 8–12 persons; seal skins and whale bones; moving camp and hunting.

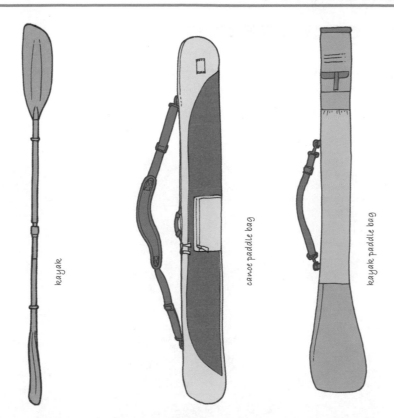

kayak

canoe paddle bag

kayak paddle bag

Haida warrior 10–20 persons; cedar or redwood logs; ceremonies.

Fur traders 7–10 persons; birch bark and wood; transporting goods.

Chippewa 1–2 persons, elm or birch bark; warcraft and used by women for hunting and gathering.

ACCESSORIES

Clothes and equipment A boat and a paddle are a great start, but you'll need some clothes to keep you comfortable on the water, and a few extras to keep you safe on your adventures.

DRYSUIT

Warm inside The quickest route to dangerous heat loss is conduction through contact with cold water. When you're paddling in very cold conditions, your best protection is a drysuit.

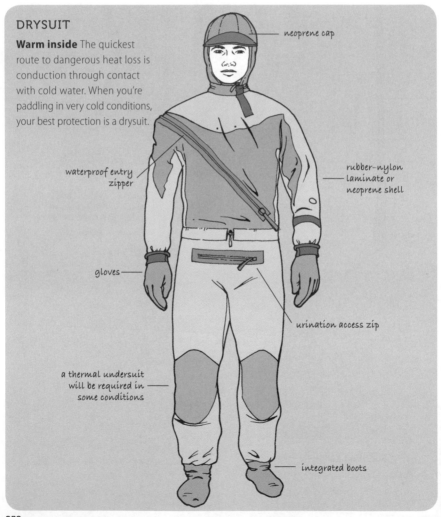

neoprene cap

waterproof entry zipper

rubber-nylon laminate or neoprene shell

gloves

urination access zip

a thermal undersuit will be required in some conditions

integrated boots

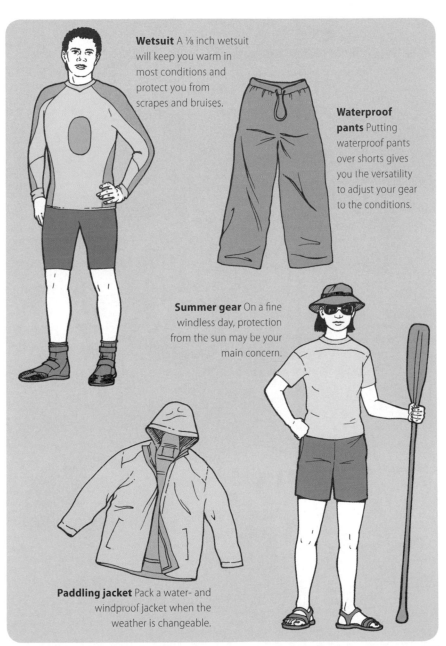

Wetsuit A ⅛ inch wetsuit will keep you warm in most conditions and protect you from scrapes and bruises.

Waterproof pants Putting waterproof pants over shorts gives you the versatility to adjust your gear to the conditions.

Summer gear On a fine windless day, protection from the sun may be your main concern.

Paddling jacket Pack a water- and windproof jacket when the weather is changeable.

253

SAFETY EQUIPMENT

Life jacket Always wear a life jacket when canoeing or kayaking. Look for an approved model that allows freedom of movement at the shoulders and neck.

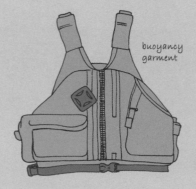

buoyancy garment

buoyancy vest

Buoyant barker It's a myth that all dogs are strong swimmers. If you're taking your pet for a paddle, consider giving it some emergency protection.

Helmets Head protection is vital when paddling in fast-moving water or surf. A helmet should fit both securely and comfortably on the head. Replace a helmet after it has received a big knock.

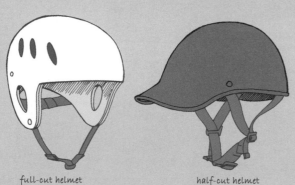

full-cut helmet

half-cut helmet

WATERPROOF CONTAINERS

dry box

barrel

dry bag

Dry inside Getting wet when paddling is unavoidable, but there is some gear that you'll want to keep dry at all times.

WATERPROOF A PLASTIC BAG

twist here

1 place your gear in the bag and press out the air

2 roll from the top of one side to the other

3 twist the rolled section over on itself

4 fold over and secure with elastic

top light for all-around visibility

Lights When you're out at night, it's important that other vessels can see you.

headlamp

inlet

outlet

Pump A pump of some sort is essential for bailing out water. Hand pumps are the simplest, but foot or electric pumps leave your hands free to do the paddling.

handle

Sea anchor A sea anchor is used in heavy seas and strong winds to keep the boat correctly oriented toward the wind. It can also be used to maintain position.

Throw bag This rescue device is designed to be an easy way of throwing a rope to someone quickly and accurately.

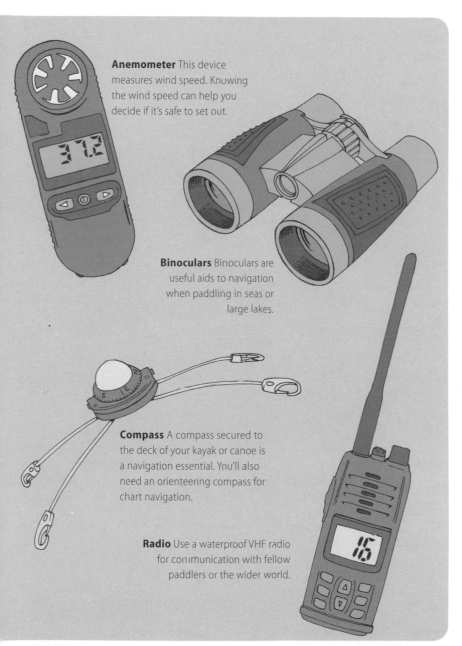

Anemometer This device measures wind speed. Knowing the wind speed can help you decide if it's safe to set out.

Binoculars Binoculars are useful aids to navigation when paddling in seas or large lakes.

Compass A compass secured to the deck of your kayak or canoe is a navigation essential. You'll also need an orienteering compass for chart navigation.

Radio Use a waterproof VHF radio for communication with fellow paddlers or the wider world.

LOADING AND TRIM

Pack a kayak Keep your heaviest items near the cockpit and away from the ends. To ensure proper trim, pack while your boat is in the water whenever you can.

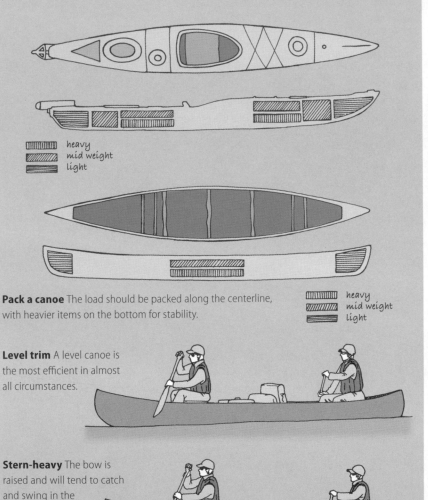

heavy
mid weight
light

Pack a canoe The load should be packed along the centerline, with heavier items on the bottom for stability.

heavy
mid weight
light

Level trim A level canoe is the most efficient in almost all circumstances.

Stern-heavy The bow is raised and will tend to catch and swing in the slightest breeze.

Skills

Get waterwise To be assured of a safe and enjoyable time in your kayak or canoe, you must know how to handle your boat in and out of the water, and know what to do when things don't go as planned.

CARRYING YOUR BOAT

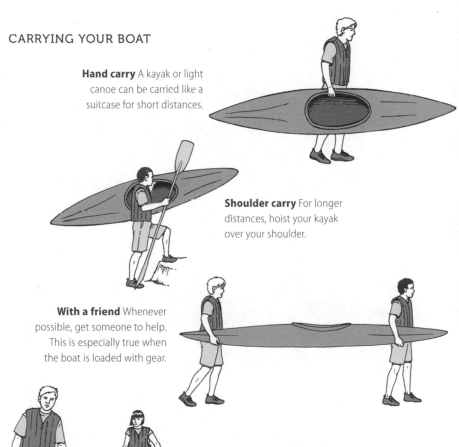

Hand carry A kayak or light canoe can be carried like a suitcase for short distances.

Shoulder carry For longer distances, hoist your kayak over your shoulder.

With a friend Whenever possible, get someone to help. This is especially true when the boat is loaded with gear.

Carry a canoe—for two Stand on the opposite side and opposite end of the canoe from your partner. Grab the closest handle or gunwale edge with your boat-side hand and lift straight upward.

PICK UP A CANOE—SOLO

1 Stand facing the side of the canoe. Grasp the gunwale, lift the canoe on its side, and take a step forward.

2 Lean forward and grasp the middle of the carrying yoke. Being careful to keep your back as straight as possible, slowly lean back and lift the canoe onto your thighs.

3 Carefully shift your forward hand to the far gunwale. Then, being sure to keep the canoe balanced, shift your back hand so that it grasps the gunwale on the near side.

4 Roll and swing the canoe over your head. This motion is easiest when it's performed quickly and smoothly.

5 Carefully lower the canoe onto your shoulders so that the yoke rests comfortably across them.

CANOE STROKES

Paddling position A standard canoe stroke uses power from body muscles—not a push–pull action with the arms. Keep your back straight and your hands properly positioned, and this action should come naturally.

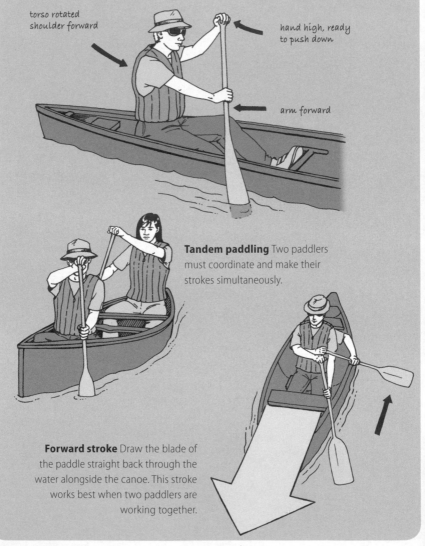

torso rotated
shoulder forward

hand high, ready
to push down

arm forward

Tandem paddling Two paddlers must coordinate and make their strokes simultaneously.

Forward stroke Draw the blade of the paddle straight back through the water alongside the canoe. This stroke works best when two paddlers are working together.

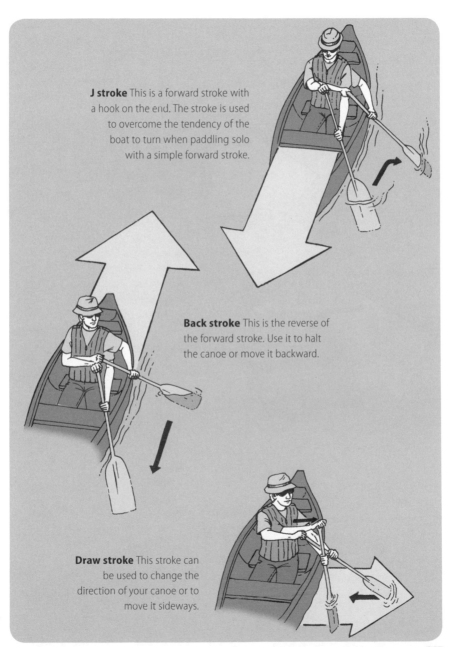

J stroke This is a forward stroke with a hook on the end. The stroke is used to overcome the tendency of the boat to turn when paddling solo with a simple forward stroke.

Back stroke This is the reverse of the forward stroke. Use it to halt the canoe or move it backward.

Draw stroke This stroke can be used to change the direction of your canoe or to move it sideways.

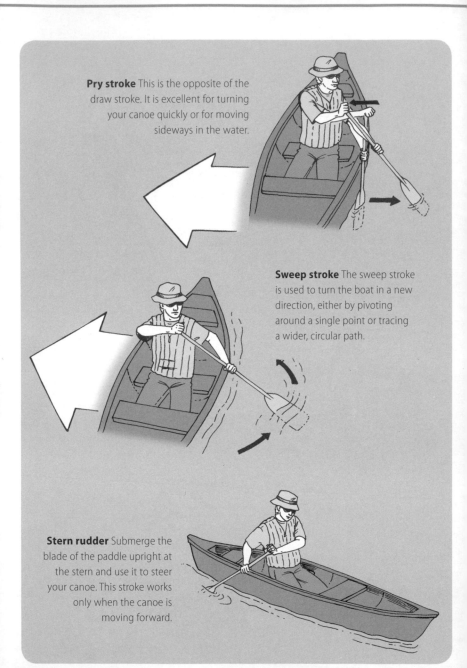

Pry stroke This is the opposite of the draw stroke. It is excellent for turning your canoe quickly or for moving sideways in the water.

Sweep stroke The sweep stroke is used to turn the boat in a new direction, either by pivoting around a single point or tracing a wider, circular path.

Stern rudder Submerge the blade of the paddle upright at the stern and use it to steer your canoe. This stroke works only when the canoe is moving forward.

KAYAK STROKE

1 Place the forward paddle blade in the water near your feet and toward the front of the kayak.

2 Rotate your torso so as to pull the blade through the water along the side of the kayak.

3 Lift the blade from the water when it passes behind your hip.

4 Continue the rotation of your torso to obtain your maximum reach on the left side of the kayak.

SCREW ROLL

Take a turn Capsizes are inevitable if you go sea or whitewater kayaking. The screw roll is the most commonly taught technique to right a capsized kayak. Learning it, or another roll sequence, is important for safety and confidence in rough waters.

1 Wait until you are upside down before beginning the roll. Lean forward, reach up, and break the surface of the water with the paddle.

2 Roll your right wrist slightly over to ensure that the face of your front paddle blade is horizontal. Now begin a smooth, sweeping motion away from the bow.

3 As the kayak begins to roll up, untwist your torso at the trunk and continue the sweep motion.

4 When the paddle reaches 90 degrees to the kayak, abruptly snap your right hip up.

5 Keep your head and body in the water until the last moment. When the boat is level, your body will follow.

WET EXIT

Out from under If you are unable to roll your kayak, you will have to do a "wet exit." If you have a spray skirt fitted, release it by yanking on the loop. Place your hands on the cockpit rim and push the kayak up, forward, and away from your legs.

EMPTY A SWAMPED BOAT

1 A swamped canoe or kayak should have sufficient flotation for it to be paddled to shallow water.

2 The boat will be heavy—don't try to lift it. Roll it onto its side and allow it to drain.

3 To empty the last of the water, raise and lower the ends of the boat like a see-saw.

Swamped solo If you are on your own, use a raised bank or slope as an aid.

Swamped on water Turn the swamped kayak over, and haul it over the deck of an upright kayak to drain.

Two to the rescue Two rescuing paddlers should move close to one another and place their paddles across their kayaks. The rescuers lift the capsized kayak over their oars and completely out of the water to drain.

WHITEWATER FREE-FLOAT POSITION

In feet first If you are swept into a rapid, don't exhaust yourself by
swimming against the current. Float on your back and keep your feet
pointed downstream.

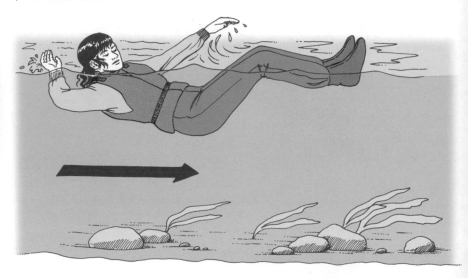

HELP POSITION

Keep your heat If you are immersed in cold
water and awaiting rescue, it is important to
keep your head above water. Adopt the HELP
position (heat escape lessening position),
which protects other areas most susceptible
to heat loss, including the armpits, sides of
the chest, groin, and the back of the knees.
If you find yourself in the water with others,
you should huddle as a group to help lessen
heat loss.

FLOAT POSITION

Relax and survive As long as you are relaxed and have air in your lungs, you will float in water. If the water is not too cold, you can survive almost indefinitely in open water by adopting the float position.

1 Float upright in the water and take a deep breath.

2 Lower your face in the water and bring your arms forward to rest at surface level. The air in your lungs will keep you floating.

3 Relax and conserve energy in this position until you need to take another breath.

4 Raise your head above the surface while you tread water. Take another breath, then return to the relaxed position.

RIVER

Go with the flow Whether you're hitching a ride on a slow drift in a gentle stream or careening down whitewater rapids, taking a boat on a river is a great way to get around.

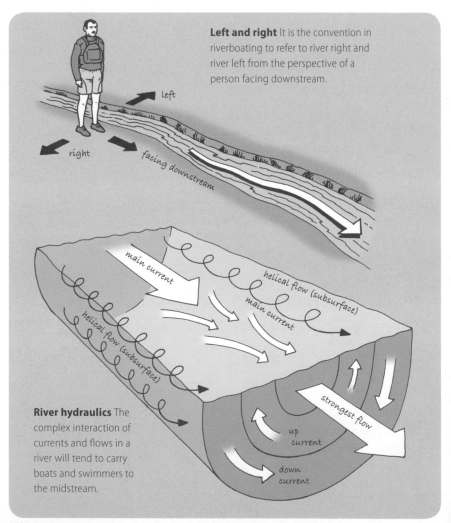

Left and right It is the convention in riverboating to refer to river right and river left from the perspective of a person facing downstream.

left

right

facing downstream

main current

helical flow (subsurface)

main current

helical flow (subsurface)

strongest flow

up current

down current

River hydraulics The complex interaction of currents and flows in a river will tend to carry boats and swimmers to the midstream.

RIVER TERMINOLOGY

A **reach** is a stretch of straight water between two bends. Even on a reach, keeping your boat going straight isn't always easy.

A **bend** is a turn in the river course. Piloting a bend with a strong current requires knowledge of several paddling strokes.

Dead water is part of the river that has no current because of erosion and changes in the river course. Dead water may have more snags and debris than fast-moving water.

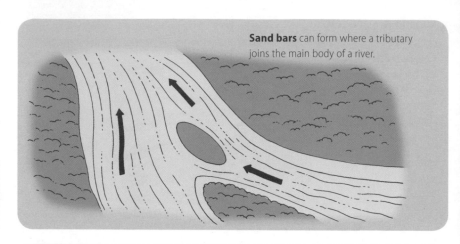

Sand bars can form where a tributary joins the main body of a river.

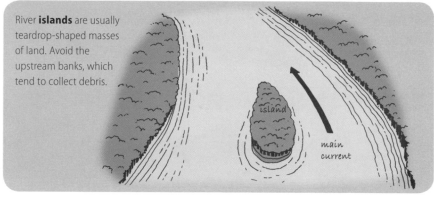

River **islands** are usually teardrop-shaped masses of land. Avoid the upstream banks, which tend to collect debris.

island

main current

The **mouth** of a river is where it discharges into a lake or ocean. The currents here are often unpredictable.

TURBULENT WATER

Staircase rapids are typical of mountain streams. The water descends in steps with little pause. For expert whitewater paddlers only.

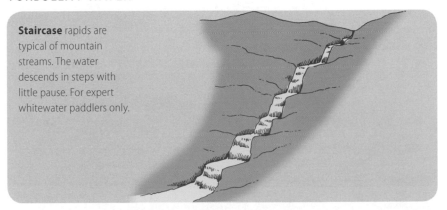

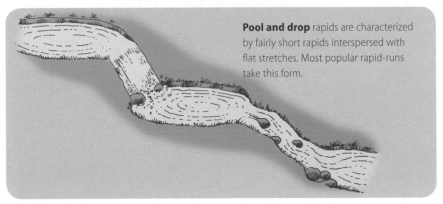

Pool and drop rapids are characterized by fairly short rapids interspersed with flat stretches. Most popular rapid-runs take this form.

Strong whirlpools and eddies form at the **confluence** of two rivers or streams.

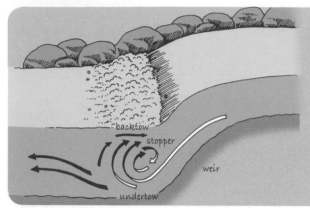

Weirs, or similar natural features where the riverbed drops suddenly, are characterized by potentially dangerous swirling currents.

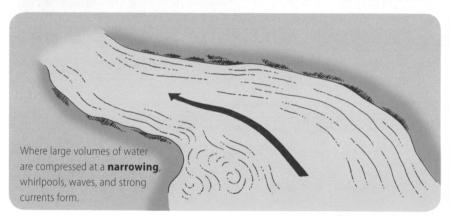

Where large volumes of water are compressed at a **narrowing**, whirlpools, waves, and strong currents form.

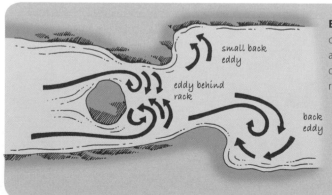

Eddies are swirling currents that form around and behind obstructions in the river's flow.

REVERSE FERRY

Driven around the bend The reverse ferry is a maneuver that moves the boat sideways across a current. It's ideal for tackling blind turns at a safe speed, and avoiding obstacles on the outside of a bend.

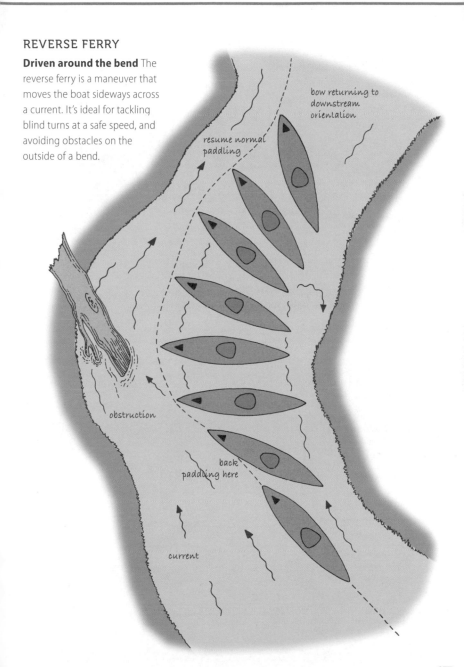

bow returning to downstream orientation

resume normal paddling

obstruction

back paddling here

current

REVERSE FERRY GLIDE

Back off This is a maneuver for moving your boat across a current. It will slow you down to give you more time as you approach danger and enable you to avoid obstacles. Begin by back paddling (**1**). Set the angle at no more than 20° (**2**). Continue to back paddle to maintain the angle (**3**) until you are ready to continue on course (**4**).

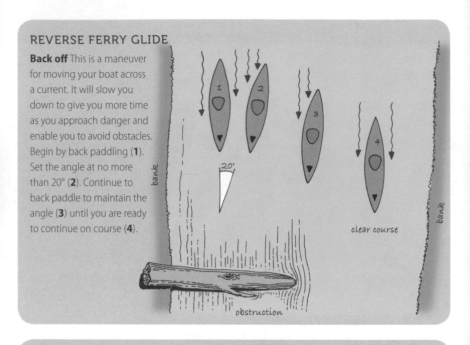

BREAK OUT

Out of the mainstream To stop your boat from continuing down the main current, use this maneuver to move into an eddy current. Approach the eddy current from upstream (**1**). Forward sweep the bow into the eddy (**2**). Edge your boat toward the inside of the turn as you enter the eddy (**3**) and finish facing upriver (**4**).

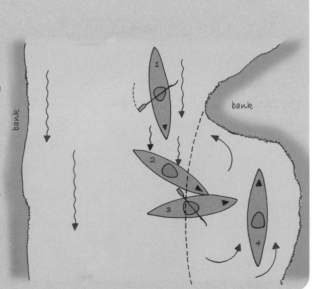

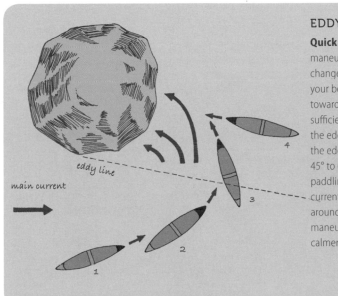

EDDY TURN

Quick turn Use this maneuver to quickly change the direction of your boat. Steer your boat toward the eddy with sufficient speed to cross the eddy line (**1**). Enter the eddy at an angle of 45° to 60° (**2**). Keep paddling while the main current swings the bow around (**3**). Plan your next maneuver while in the calmer waters (**4**).

eddy line

main current

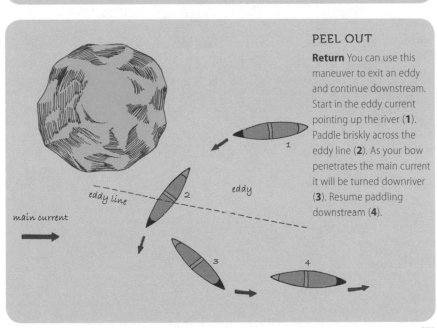

PEEL OUT

Return You can use this maneuver to exit an eddy and continue downstream. Start in the eddy current pointing up the river (**1**). Paddle briskly across the eddy line (**2**). As your bow penetrates the main current it will be turned downriver (**3**). Resume paddling downstream (**4**).

eddy line

eddy

main current

RIVER SIGNALS

Get the message Rivers—especially fast-flowing ones—can be noisy places. In order to communicate, canoeists and kayakers have developed an internationally recognized set of signals, using arms and paddles.

go (paddle signal)

stop (hand signal)

go (hand signal)

stop (paddle signal)

stop this side

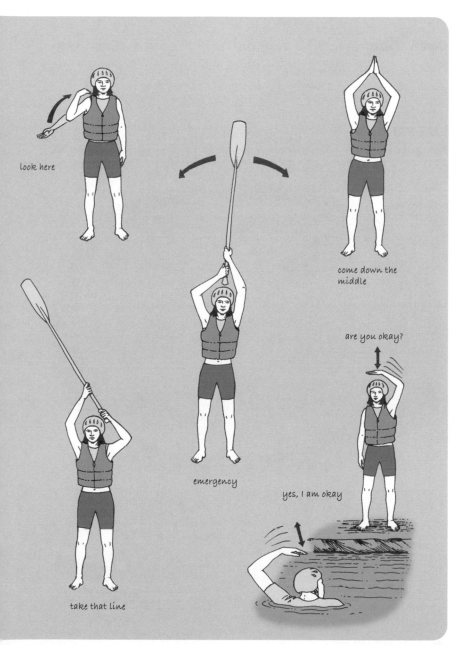

look here

come down the middle

take that line

emergency

are you okay?

yes, I am okay

Lake and Sea

Open water Canoeing or kayaking over large, open bodies of water presents quite different challenges from river boating. Gain experience and confidence, and you can truly explore.

LAKE WIND

Wind and waves Wind across a large, open area of water can easily blow the unwary paddler off course. Onshore winds blowing across a large lake can cause choppy waters and waves big enough to swamp your canoe.

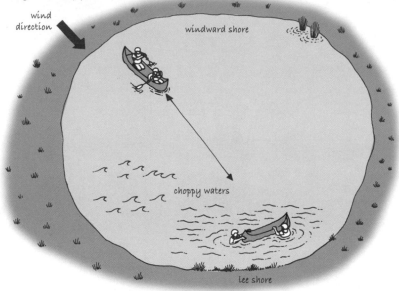

wind direction

windward shore

choppy waters

lee shore

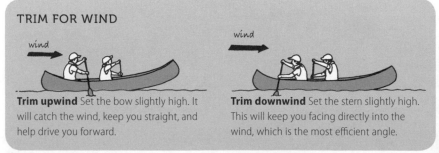

TRIM FOR WIND

wind

Trim upwind Set the bow slightly high. It will catch the wind, keep you straight, and help drive you forward.

wind

Trim downwind Set the stern slightly high. This will keep you facing directly into the wind, which is the most efficient angle.

SAIL

Wind-assisted Rather than battling the wind, you can take advantage of it with the addition of a canoe or kayak sail system. There are many possibilities, including windsurfer rigs, parafoil kites, and spinnakers.

FERRY ANGLE

Drift To compensate for the effects of wind and currents when crossing a large body of water, don't aim for your destination. Instead, set your boat at an angle.

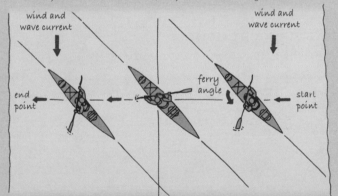

wind and wave current

wind and wave current

end point

ferry angle

start point

Tides The tides are greatest during full and new moons, when the Sun and Moon are aligned either on the same or opposite sides of Earth.

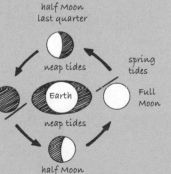

half Moon last quarter

neap tides

spring tides

new Moon

spring tides

Earth

Full Moon

neap tides

half Moon first quarter

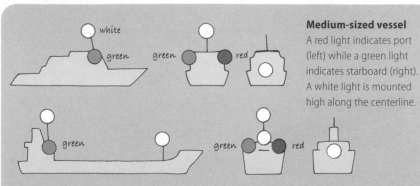

Medium-sized vessel
A red light indicates port (left) while a green light indicates starboard (right). A white light is mounted high along the centerline.

Large vessel Vessels longer than 164 feet must have two white lights—one set high near the stern, and another lower down near the bow.

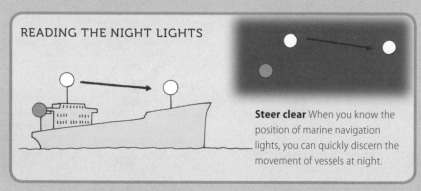

READING THE NIGHT LIGHTS

Steer clear When you know the position of marine navigation lights, you can quickly discern the movement of vessels at night.

Give way rules Use your common sense when paddling among other watercraft. Kayaks and canoes are small—never assume that you have been seen. Steer clear of large vessels that can be restricted in their ability to stop or turn. The two most important rules to remember are: keep right of oncoming vessels; and give way to a vessel approaching from starboard.

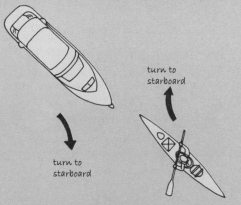

turn to starboard

turn to starboard

NAVIGATING

Transits A transit is the line formed by the lining up of two features, for example a lighthouse and a buoy. Transits are of great use in sea kayaking. When you are plotting your course on your chart, locate as many transits as possible and draw them on the chart.

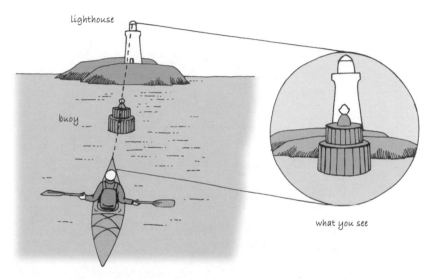

lighthouse

buoy

what you see

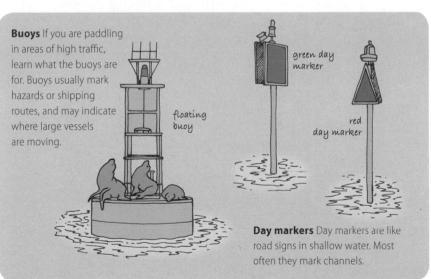

Buoys If you are paddling in areas of high traffic, learn what the buoys are for. Buoys usually mark hazards or shipping routes, and may indicate where large vessels are moving.

floating buoy

green day marker

red day marker

Day markers Day markers are like road signs in shallow water. Most often they mark channels.

WEATHER

The moods and vagaries of weather fascinate and frighten us, thrill and threaten us. A little knowledge of what drives weather will help keep you safe outdoors, and add to your appreciation of nature's nonstop show.

WEATHER FUNDAMENTALS

The weather engine Fueled by the heat of the Sun, the atmosphere that surrounds Earth is in a constant state of flux, subject to variations in temperature, wind, pressure, humidity, and precipitation.

THE SUN AND THE SEASONS

Tilted planet Because Earth's axis is tilted at an angle of 23.5 degrees, the amount of solar energy that reaches different parts of the globe varies as the planet orbits the Sun. These variations create our seasons, which are opposite in the northern and southern hemispheres.

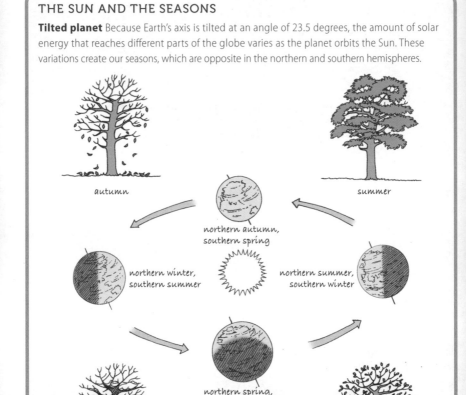

autumn

summer

northern autumn,
southern spring

northern winter,
southern summer

northern summer,
southern winter

northern spring,
southern autumn

winter

spring

ATMOSPHERE

Layers Earth's atmosphere consists of distinct layers that are characterized by their temperature profiles. The lowest layer is the troposphere, which accounts for 90 percent of the atmosphere's total mass. It is here that we enjoy Earth's mostly temperate climate and experience weather.

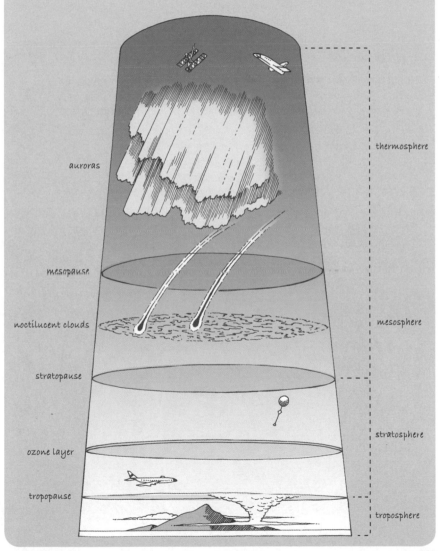

thermosphere

auroras

mesopause

noctilucent clouds

mesosphere

stratopause

stratosphere

ozone layer

tropopause

troposphere

AIR IN MOTION

Wind Currents of air—winds—are caused by differences in air pressure. These differences occur because solar radiation is not uniform across the planet, nor is the ability of surfaces to absorb or reflect solar energy the same.

GLOBAL WINDS

Cells, jets, and trade winds Because hot air rises and cold air sinks, the Sun's uneven heating of Earth's surface causes air to circulate in large cells. These patterns of air circulation are deflected by the planet's rotation, and form Earth's major wind systems.

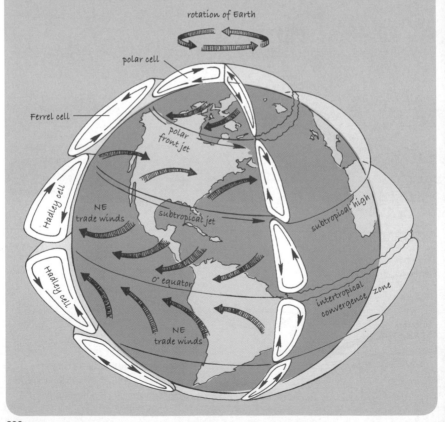

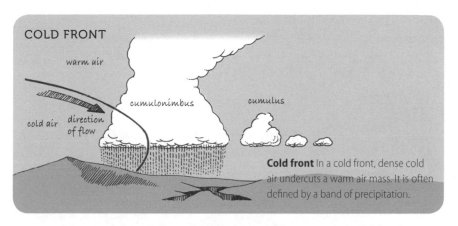

COLD FRONT

warm air

cumulonimbus

cumulus

cold air   direction of flow

Cold front In a cold front, dense cold air undercuts a warm air mass. It is often defined by a band of precipitation.

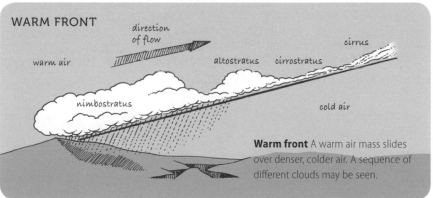

WARM FRONT

direction of flow

cirrus

warm air

altostratus   cirrostratus

nimbostratus

cold air

Warm front A warm air mass slides over denser, colder air. A sequence of different clouds may be seen.

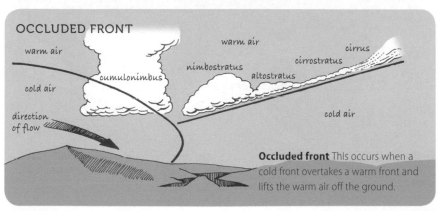

OCCLUDED FRONT

warm air

warm air

cirrus

cold air

nimbostratus   cirrostratus

altostratus

cumulonimbus

direction of flow

cold air

Occluded front This occurs when a cold front overtakes a warm front and lifts the warm air off the ground.

MIDLATITUDE VARIABILITY

Shifting flow Variable weather in the midlatitudes is generated by low-pressure storms traveling from west to east. Sometimes blocking occurs when air masses stall, and weather does not change for days, or even weeks, at a time.

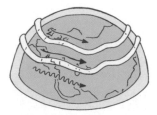

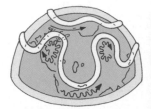

Troughs Powerful planetary waves can distort jet streams, and carry cold air to low latitudes and warm air to high latitudes, creating severe weather.

Normal Regular, slightly meandering polar jet streams bring variable weather patterns to the midlatitudes without causing extreme conditions.

Blocking High- and low-pressure areas may be cut off. Stationary systems may cause flooding, extended cold spells, heat waves, and drought.

SEA BREEZES

Day breeze A closed circulation forms as cooled air from over the water rushes onshore to replace rising warm air, which then descends back toward the sea.

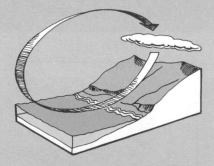

Night breeze Overnight, land cools quickly, but sea surface temperatures remain virtually unchanged. Cooler air drains off the land and over the sea.

TOPOGRAPHIC WINDS

Valley day During the day, sunlit slopes warm up, driving a slight breeze uphill. The air eventually subsides and warms during descent.

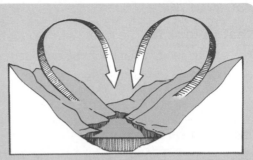

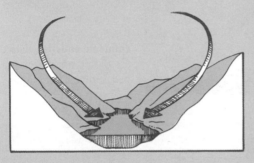

Valley night At night, cooled soil chills the overlaying air, which then flows down the slopes and accumulates in the valley, creating a downward breeze.

Foehn wind These winds develop when air is forced to cross a mountain. During ascent, air is cooled and moisture condenses. If precipitation is released, the now-dry air descends on the leeward side and warms.

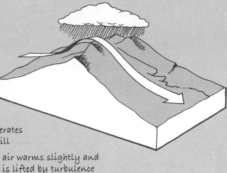

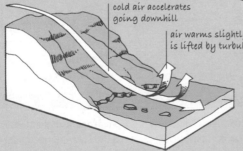

cold air accelerates going downhill

air warms slightly and is lifted by turbulence

Katabatic These intense winds form when cold air, which is denser than warm air, flows downhill. Driven by gravity, the wind strength depends on the height of the drop.

Types of Clouds

What to look for Clouds are an important indicator not only of current weather, but also of what might be expected over the next few hours or even days. Keep watching the sky!

IDENTIFICATION OF CLOUDS

Cumulus (far left) surface to 40,000 ft; vertical puffy white or gray with flat base.

Cumulonimbus (left) surface to 40,000 ft; indicative of thunderstorms.

Cirrus 15,000 to 40,000 ft; long, wispy streams composed of ice.

Cirrocumulus 15,000 to 40,000 ft—called "mackerel sky"—indicates cold weather.

Cirrostratus 15,000 to 40,000 ft; high, sheetlike, thin clouds covering entire sky.

Altocumulus 6,500 ft to 20,000 ft; grayish-white with one part darker; coming storm.

Stratus surface to 6,500 ft; low, uniform, gray; covering most of sky, like a high fog.

Stratocumulus surface to 6,500 ft; low, lumpy, gray; in lines or spread out; light rain.

294

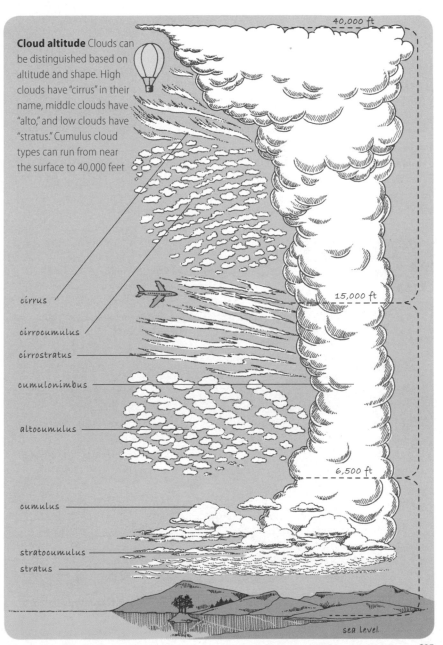

Cloud altitude Clouds can be distinguished based on altitude and shape. High clouds have "cirrus" in their name, middle clouds have "alto," and low clouds have "stratus." Cumulus cloud types can run from near the surface to 40,000 feet

40,000 ft

15,000 ft

6,500 ft

cirrus

cirrocumulus

cirrostratus

cumulonimbus

altocumulus

cumulus

stratocumulus

stratus

sea level

1 A cloud begins when air rises by convection over ground heated by the Sun. As it rises, the temperature drops, and nears the condensation level.

2 Above the condensation level, water vapor condenses into droplets on tiny particles, or cloud condensation nuclei, forming a cumulus cloud.

3 The cloud drifts away, carried by the wind. If the ground below remains hot, a new convective cloud may form in the same way.

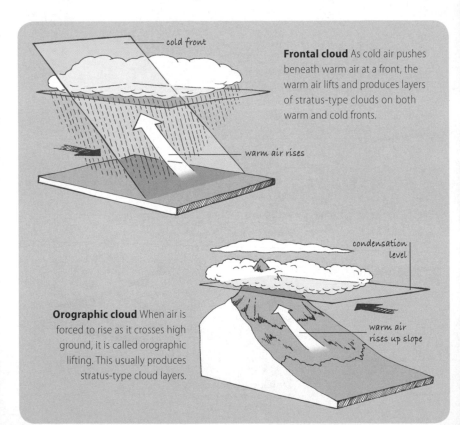

Frontal cloud As cold air pushes beneath warm air at a front, the warm air lifts and produces layers of stratus-type clouds on both warm and cold fronts.

Orographic cloud When air is forced to rise as it crosses high ground, it is called orographic lifting. This usually produces stratus-type cloud layers.

Fog

Cloud all around Fog is really cloud that forms near the ground, and, like cloud, develops as a result of condensation. Fog usually consists of water droplets that adhere to atmospheric particles, such as dust specks.

Types of fog Fog usually forms when humid air is cooled to its dew point, causing water vapor to condense into tiny drops. Less often, evaporation of water into air can play a role. The illustrations below show four common ways that fog can form.

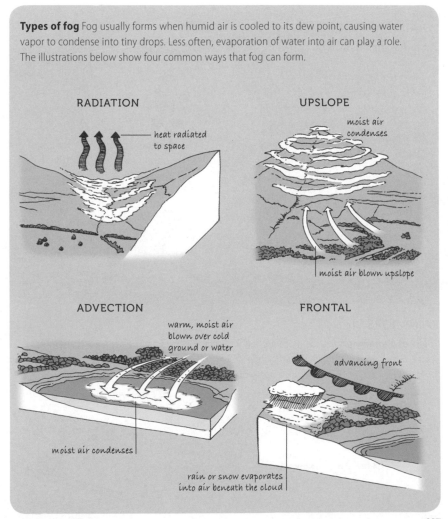

RADIATION

heat radiated to space

UPSLOPE

moist air condenses

moist air blown upslope

ADVECTION

warm, moist air blown over cold ground or water

moist air condenses

FRONTAL

advancing front

rain or snow evaporates into air beneath the cloud

PRECIPITATION

Rain, hail, snow, and sleet Any of the various forms of water that fall from the atmosphere and reach the ground are called precipitation. It's something that you always have to be prepared for in the outdoors.

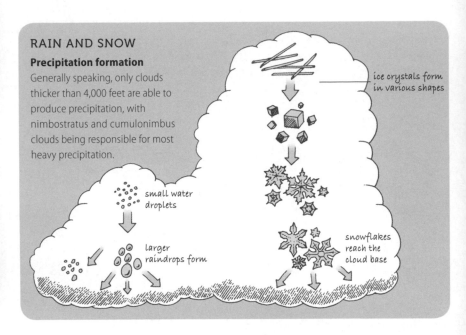

RAIN AND SNOW

Precipitation formation
Generally speaking, only clouds thicker than 4,000 feet are able to produce precipitation, with nimbostratus and cumulonimbus clouds being responsible for most heavy precipitation.

ice crystals form in various shapes

small water droplets

larger raindrops form

snowflakes reach the cloud base

RAINDROPS

Shape of a raindrop Small raindrops are spherical, while large raindrops attain an oblate spheroid shape, with a flattened or indented bottom due to air resistance. Raindrops that are larger still will open up like a parachute before bursting.

0.05 inch
spherical

0.08 inch
flattened

0.12 inch
indented

>0.18 inch
parachute

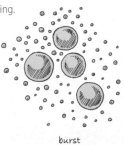
burst

SNOW CRYSTALS

Snowflake shapes Snowflakes take many different forms but all are variations of a basic hexagonal crystal shape. The shape of the flake depends on the temperature and humidity within the cloud in which it forms.

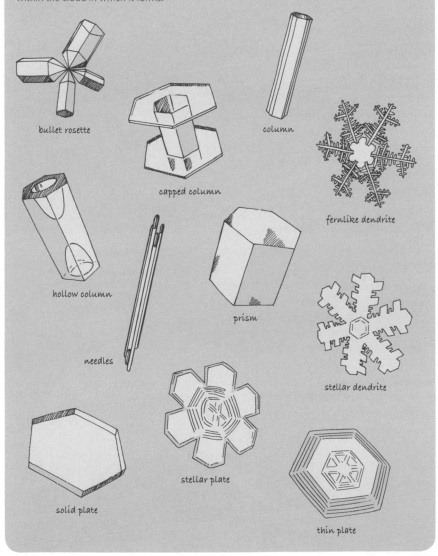

bullet rosette

capped column

column

fernlike dendrite

hollow column

needles

prism

stellar dendrite

solid plate

stellar plate

thin plate

LAKE EFFECT SNOW

Snowy shore When extremely cold winds move across warmer lake water, vapor is picked up and later deposited as heavy snow on the lee shore. Lake-effect snow is common up to 50 miles to the east of North America's Great Lakes in early winter, before the lakes freeze.

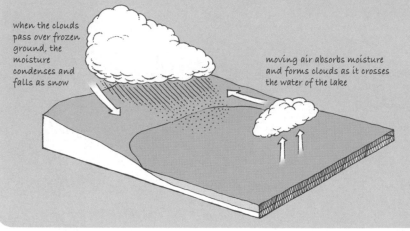

when the clouds pass over frozen ground, the moisture condenses and falls as snow

moving air absorbs moisture and forms clouds as it crosses the water of the lake

TOO COLD TO SNOW?

A cold conundrum Snow becomes less likely at temperatures well below freezing. Very cold air cannot hold much water vapor. Cold air is also dense and heavy, and therefore less likely to be lifted to expand and condense to form snow.

strong mountain airflow may lift cold air but even if ice crystals form, they are likely to sublimate in the dry air as they fall

saturated air at 0°F contains about one-quarter of the water vapor as at 32°F

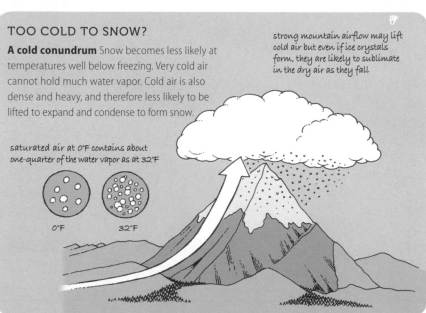

0°F   32°F

GRAUPEL, HAIL, AND ICE PELLETS

Solid ice precipitation Ice particles formed in the atmosphere often reach the ground before melting. Graupel and hailstones grow from smaller particles. Ice pellets are raindrops that freeze while on their way to the ground.

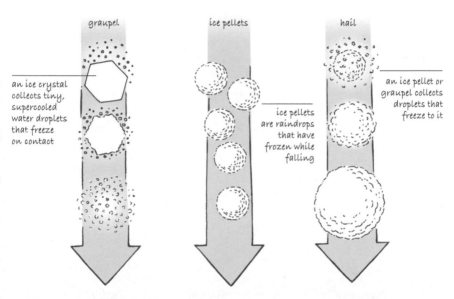

graupel

ice pellets

hail

an ice crystal collects tiny, supercooled water droplets that freeze on contact

ice pellets are raindrops that have frozen while falling

an ice pellet or graupel collects droplets that freeze to it

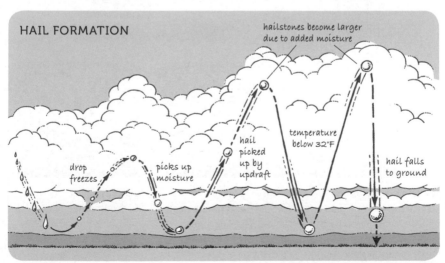

HAIL FORMATION

hailstones become larger due to added moisture

drop freezes

picks up moisture

hail picked up by updraft

temperature below 32°F

hail falls to ground

DANGEROUS CONDITIONS

Danger above Whether it be floods, fires, blizzards, or lightning, severe weather is the number one killer in the outdoors. Learn to recognize signs of bad weather before it catches you unaware.

THUNDERSTORMS

Light and sound Thunderstorms are one of nature's most awesome phenomena. They are also potentially dangerous. If you're outside and one is brewing, seek shelter.

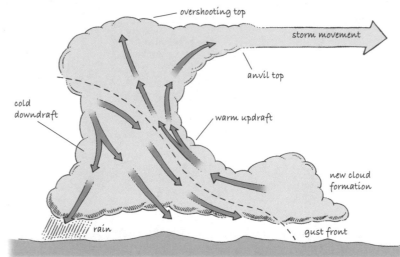

STAGES OF A THUNDERSTORM

Towering cumulus Condensing water to make the cloud heats the air. Updrafts prevail within the cloud and the cloud rapidly rises.

Mature The updraft spreads out where it strikes the stable stratosphere. A downdraft forms where air is cooled. Precipitation begins falling.

Dissipating Soon, downdrafts predominate, the supply of warm air is shut off, and the cloud dissipates. Typical storms last less than an hour.

LIGHTNING

Intracloud lightning
The most common type of lightning is an arc between upper and lower parts of a cloud that have an opposite charge.

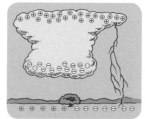

Cloud to ground positive polarity This lightning strike connects the positive charge high in the thunderstorm and a negative charge in the ground beneath.

Cloud to ground negative polarity This lightning strike connects the negative charge at the bottom of the thunderstorm and the positive charge in the ground beneath.

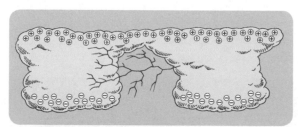

Intercloud A less common discharge is between adjacent clouds, when their areas of opposite charge are located close to each other.

Hair-raising If you feel a tingling on the skin or your hair stands on end, you are in grave danger. Get to shelter straight away or adopt the lightning crouch (see right).

Lightning crouch Put your feet together, squat down, tuck your head, and cover your ears. You'll make yourself a small target, and any ground current should pass through your feet and not your torso.

LIGHTNING: PLACES TO AVOID

High ground If you are heading toward high ground and a storm is developing, turn back.

Lone tree It may be tempting, but do not seek shelter under an isolated tree. It will attract lightning and the trunk may explode if the tree is struck.

Picnic shelter A small open-sided picnic shelter does not offer any protection.

LIGHTNING: PLACES TO BE

Grove A dense grove of low trees is relatively safe, especially if there are much higher trees at a distance.

Car Get to an enclosed building or car if you can. Roll up all the windows, and do not touch anything metal.

Down low A gully or ditch will offer some protection, but beware of the risk of flash flooding.

TORNADOES

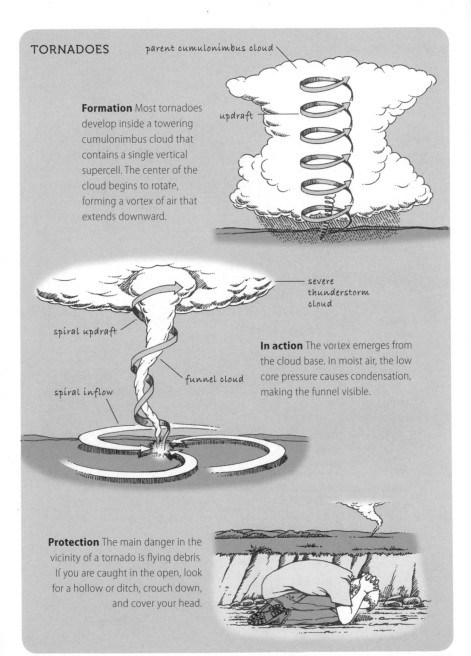

parent cumulonimbus cloud

updraft

Formation Most tornadoes develop inside a towering cumulonimbus cloud that contains a single vertical supercell. The center of the cloud begins to rotate, forming a vortex of air that extends downward.

severe thunderstorm cloud

spiral updraft

funnel cloud

spiral inflow

In action The vortex emerges from the cloud base. In moist air, the low core pressure causes condensation, making the funnel visible.

Protection The main danger in the vicinity of a tornado is flying debris. If you are caught in the open, look for a hollow or ditch, crouch down, and cover your head.

FOREST FIRES

Land ablaze Forest fires, or wildfires, are a danger in any densely vegetated area that experiences hot, dry, and windy weather. When these conditions occur, postpone any excursions into fire-prone areas. If you are already outdoors, find a safe place and wait it out.

Heat shield The biggest killer in a forest fire is radiant heat. Cover up with natural fiber clothing and blankets, and seek the shelter of something solid, like a group of boulders.

Water Get into a lake or dam. Protect yourself from radiant heat and smoke with sodden clothes or blankets.

Clearing A clearing or similar natural firebreak can act as a refuge. Again, protection from radiant heat and smoke will be the key to survival.

Make a break Starve an approaching fire front of fuel by setting fire to the vegetation downwind. This will provide a fire break and some degree of safety.

SAND AND DUST STORMS

Sandblasted Prolonged dry weather, high temperatures, and strong winds can cause blinding sand and dust storms that are hazardous to health, drastically reduce visibility, and make life in the open very difficult. They are most frequent in deserts, but can occur elsewhere.

Be prepared Pack swimming goggles and a dust mask if you are traveling in a region where dust storms are likely.

Face protection The inhabitants of dusty North Africa and the Middle East never leave home without some ready protection.

Sit it out Seek elevated ground where the concentration of blown sand is reduced. Get behind a windbreak if possible, such as a boulder or a compliant camel.

WEATHER MAPS

Window on the weather Weather maps (or charts) are the main tools of meteorology. A synoptic chart is a snapshot of an area's weather at any given time; a prognostic chart predicts future weather.

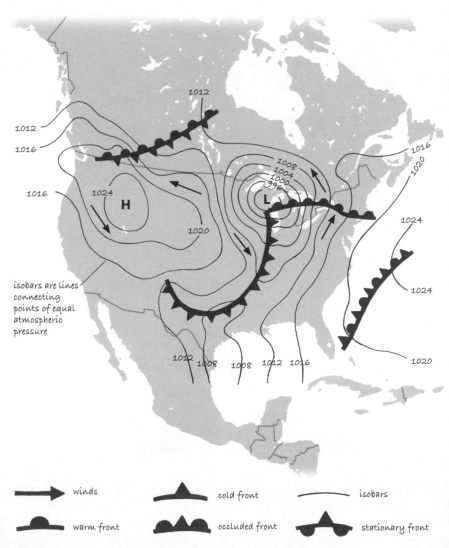

1012

1012

1016

1016

1024

H

1020

1008
1004
1000
996

L

1016

1020

1024

1024

isobars are lines
connecting
points of equal
atmospheric
pressure

1012 1008   1008   1012 1016

1020

→ winds

cold front

isobars

warm front

occluded front

stationary front

METEOROLOGICAL SYMBOLS

Reading the signs Meteorologists use symbols to describe wind, precipitation, and cloud patterns. They form part of an international shorthand and are marked on meteorologists' working charts, but do not usually appear on media presentations.

CURRENT WEATHER

light drizzle	steady, light drizzle	intermittent, moderate drizzle	steady, moderate drizzle	intermittent, heavy drizzle	steady, heavy drizzle	light rain
steady, light rain	intermittent, moderate rain	steady, moderate rain	intermittent, heavy rain	steady, heavy rain	light snow	steady, light snow
intermittent, moderate snow	steady, moderate snow	intermittent, heavy snow	steady, heavy snow	hail	freezing rain	smoke
tornado	dust storm	fog	thunderstorm	lightning	hurricane	

CLOUDS

stratus	cumulus	nimbostratus	stratocumulus	altostratus	altocumulus
cirrus	cirrostratus	cirrocumulus	cumulonimbus calvus	cumulonimbus with anvil	

WIND SPEED KNOTS (MPH)

calm	1-2	3-7	8-12	13-17	18-22	48-52	103-107

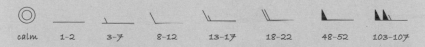

WEATHER LORE

Natural signs For millennia, people have observed links between weather, the state of the sky, and the behavior of plants and animals. Weather lore developed as a curious mix of common sense and superstition.

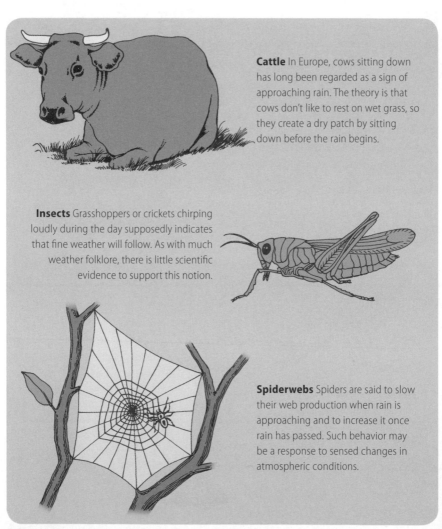

Cattle In Europe, cows sitting down has long been regarded as a sign of approaching rain. The theory is that cows don't like to rest on wet grass, so they create a dry patch by sitting down before the rain begins.

Insects Grasshoppers or crickets chirping loudly during the day supposedly indicates that fine weather will follow. As with much weather folklore, there is little scientific evidence to support this notion.

Spiderwebs Spiders are said to slow their web production when rain is approaching and to increase it once rain has passed. Such behavior may be a response to sensed changes in atmospheric conditions.

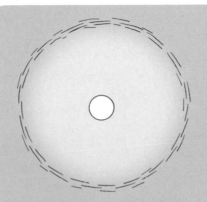

Halo The ethereal ring sometimes seen around the Sun or Moon is caused by the bending of light through a thin veil of ice-crystal cloud. This formation sometimes runs ahead of a cold front, and cold fronts can certainly generate rain.

Trees Pine cones are highly sensitive to changes in atmospheric moisture levels: they close when humidity is high and open when humidity is low. High humidity levels are often associated with the onset of rain.

Smoke Campfire smoke rises straight up when there is no wind. Still air is generally stable and won't move moisture into an area, meaning good weather will continue or arrive soon.

Flowers When the humidity rises and rain is more likely, many flowers close their petals so rain doesn't wash away their pollen.

MAPS AND NAVIGATION

You might want to get into the wilderness to get away from it all, but you will still want to know exactly where you are. Good maps and a compass will keep you grounded.

Maps

Your world on the page If you venture into the wild with a good map and the knowledge of how to use it, you need never get lost. The important things to learn are the geographic coordinates, map scale, and contour lines.

FOLD A MAP

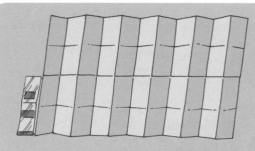

1 Start with your map completely open. Study the creases of the map, if they are fresh, they will indicate the correct folding sequence.

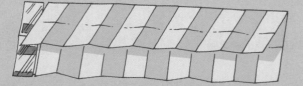

2 Fold the map in half by bringing the top edge to meet the bottom edge.

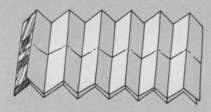

3 Fold the map inward, accordion-style, making sure to keep the map cover on top.

4 Finally, fold the map over with the cover on top. Some maps have a third section that needs to be tucked in.

MAP READER WHEELS

Analog These devices display distance by means of needle and dial printed with various map scales.

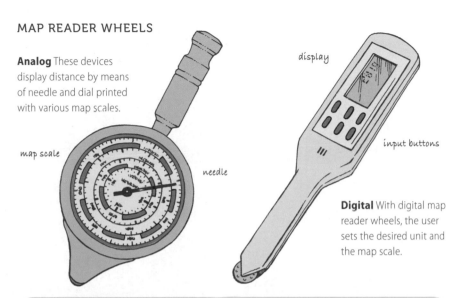

display

map scale

needle

input buttons

Digital With digital map reader wheels, the user sets the desired unit and the map scale.

CONTOUR LINES

Lines and landforms
Contour lines are the key to reading topographic maps. Every hiker should be able to "read" the lines on the map and instantly get a mental picture of the landscape it represents. Put simply, each contour line on a map connects points where the ground is the same height. Lines close together indicate steep slopes. Spaces between lines or lines far apart indicate flat or gently sloping ground.

200 ft

150 ft

100 ft

50 ft

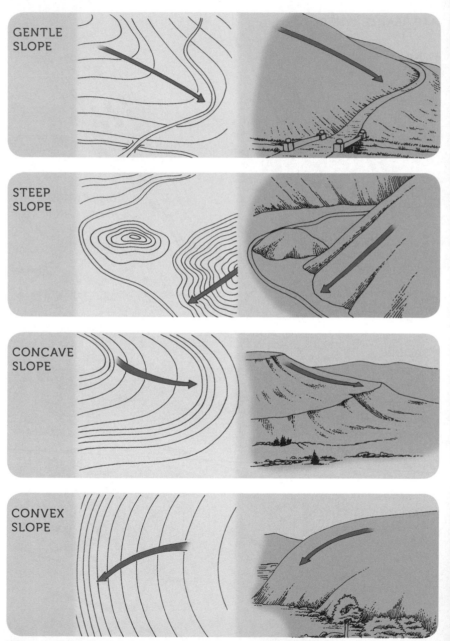

GENTLE SLOPE

STEEP SLOPE

CONCAVE SLOPE

CONVEX SLOPE

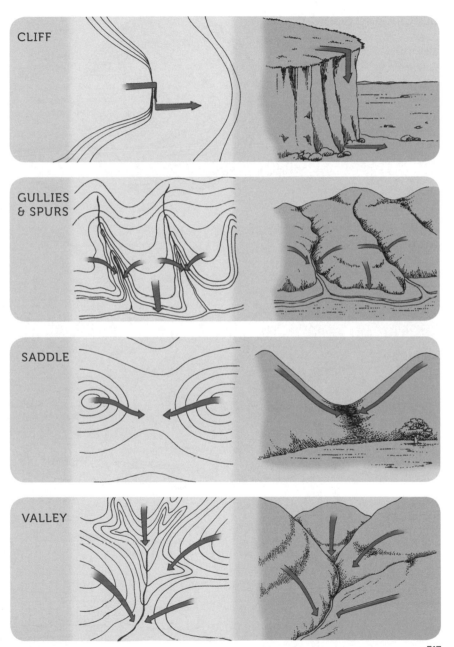

CLIFF

GULLIES & SPURS

SADDLE

VALLEY

GEOGRAPHIC COORDINATES

Global grid By drawing a set of east–west rings around the world (lines of latitude, parallel to the Equator) and a set of lines drawn between the poles (lines of longitude), a grid is formed from which any location on Earth's surface can be located.

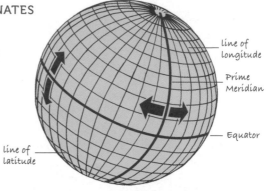

line of longitude

Prime Meridian

Equator

line of latitude

MAP PROJECTIONS

The mapping conundrum Earth is spherical, but maps are flat. In order to create a flat map, cartographers have to stretch and squash segments of the globe.

spherical Earth

Projections The different ways cartographers "flatten" Earth are known as projections.

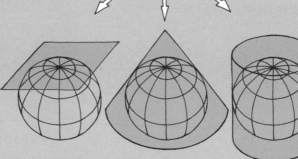

planar   conical   cylindrical

Grid Fortunately the grid distortions at the scale of hiking maps are too minor to cause much of a headache.

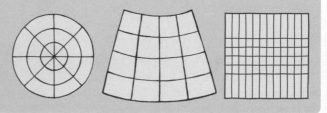

MAGNETIC EARTH

Finding north Our planet is one big magnet. That fact can be turned to your advantage for precise navigation—just as long as you have a map, a compass, and an understanding of how magnetic north and true north differ.

MAGNETIC NORTH

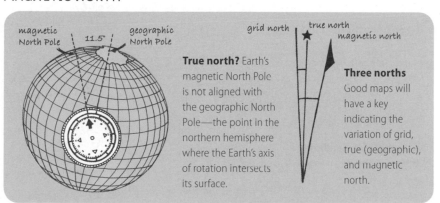

True north? Earth's magnetic North Pole is not aligned with the geographic North Pole—the point in the northern hemisphere where the Earth's axis of rotation intersects its surface.

Three norths Good maps will have a key indicating the variation of grid, true (geographic), and magnetic north.

DECLINATION

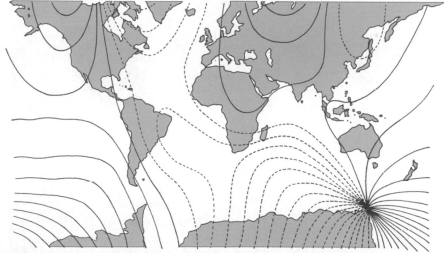

Declination map Because of distortions in the magnetic field, the alignment of a compass needle varies from place to place. The difference between local magnetic north and true north is known as declination.

319

Compass

Your wayfinder The Chinese invented the compass about a thousand years ago, and even in the age of satellite-aided navigation, compass skills are essential for the outdoors adventurer.

ORIENTEERING COMPASS

Plastic fantastic This type of compass sits on a transparent baseplate and is designed to be used in conjunction with a topographical map. It is the most versatile type of compass for outdoor use, and is sufficient for almost any situation.

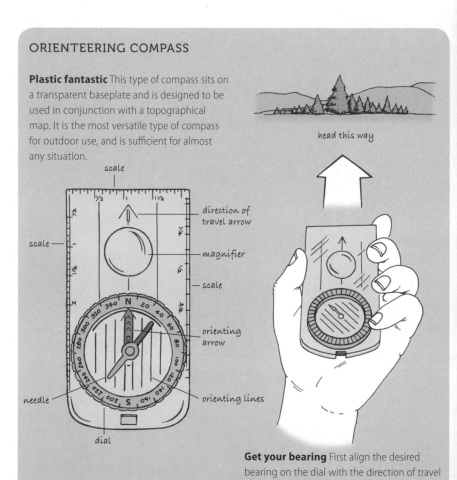

head this way

scale

scale

direction of travel arrow

magnifier

scale

orienting arrow

orienting lines

needle

dial

Get your bearing First align the desired bearing on the dial with the direction of travel arrow. Then hold the compass in front of you and turn until the north end of the compass needle is directly over the orienting arrow.

ORIENT A MAP

Line it up Align the edge of your compass with the north–south lines of your map. Set the dial of your compass to north, taking into account magnetic deviation in your area (this information will be printed on your map). Turn the map and compass together until the north (red) end of the compass needle is directly over the orienting arrow. Your map is now correctly oriented.

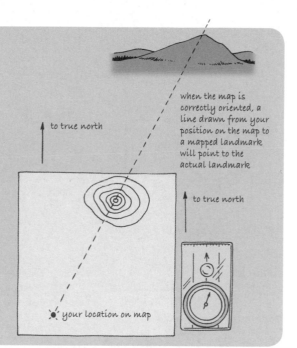

when the map is correctly oriented, a line drawn from your position on the map to a mapped landmark will point to the actual landmark

to true north

to true north

your location on map

TAKE A BEARING

Which way to go Your map does not have to be oriented to take a bearing. Place the compass on the map with the edge along the line of travel. Rotate the dial until the "N" is aligned with map north and the orienting lines are parallel with the north–south lines on the map. The bearing on the dial is the bearing you should follow. Remember to make allowances for magnetic declination.

92   93   94   95   96

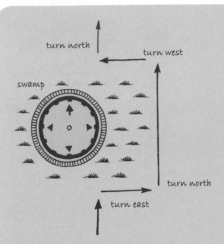

Basic bypass This bypass involves three 90-degree turns with a fourth to bring you back on track. For accuracy, count your paces when bypassing.

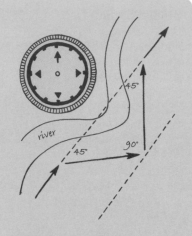

45- and 90-degree bypass This bypass involves just three turns. Count your paces to ensure that each length is of equal distance.

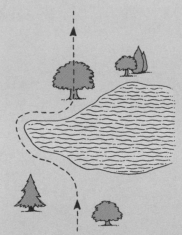

Marker Bypassing is easy if you can see a feature beyond the obstacle aligned with your bearing. In this case walk around the lake until you reach the lone tree.

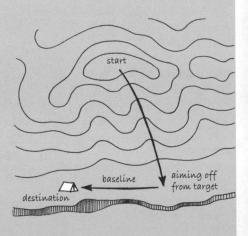

Deliberate offset Take a bearing left or right of your final objective. That way, when you hit a "baseline," such as a road or river, you know which way to turn.

MIRRORED SIGHTING COMPASS

Mirror assisted This compass type is similar to an orienteering compass with the addition of a hinged mirror. This allows you to sight your target and your bearing at the same time.

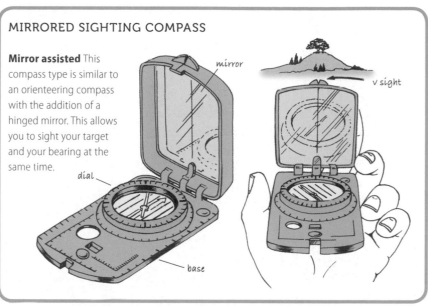

mirror

v sight

dial

base

LENSATIC COMPASS

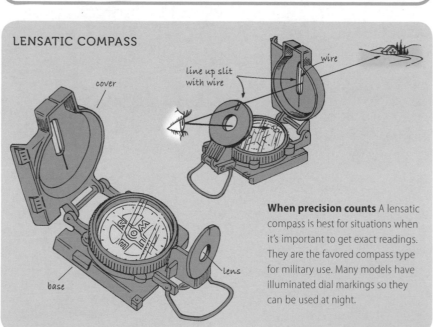

cover

line up slit with wire

wire

lens

base

When precision counts A lensatic compass is best for situations when it's important to get exact readings. They are the favored compass type for military use. Many models have illuminated dial markings so they can be used at night.

Thumb compass These thumb-mounted compasses are used in orienteering.

Direct sighting Look through the eyepiece to get a bearing accurate to within one degree.

Button A compass doesn't have to be big to be useful. Keep a little one in reserve.

MAKE A COMPASS

Magnetize To make a compass, first magnetize a needle by stroking it in one direction with a magnet. If you stroke toward the point of your needle, the point will indicate north.

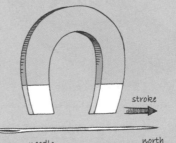

stroke

needle

north

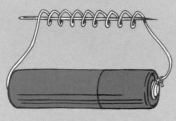

insulated wire

Battery method Alternatively, you can magnetize a needle by coiling some insulated wire around it. Connect the wire to a battery for about five to ten minutes.

battery

mug

Now you know If you gently lower the needle into a mug of water, surface tension should keep it floating (a coating of natural oil from your hair will help). The sharp end will point toward magnetic north.

GPS

Help from above Hand-held GPS units are a fantastic aid to navigation. However, they are no substitute for a map, and you should always carry a compass and know how to use it in case of equipment failure.

the surface of this sphere represents all possible locations when measured against satellite 1

satellite 2

satellite 1

satellite 3

The Global Positioning System

A GPS unit works by measuring its exact distance from a minimum of three satellites. Its location is where three spheres of radius, given by the distance to each of three satellites, intersect at Earth's surface.

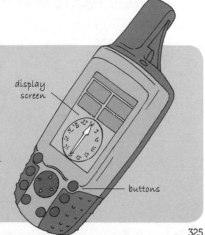

HAND-HELD UNIT

Pocket wonder A hand-held GPS unit will inform you of your location, speed, and approximate altitude. It will also permit you to retrace your path, guide you to specific waypoints, and will work as a compass as long as you are moving in one direction. The more expensive models come with built-in maps, electronic compasses, and barometers.

display screen

buttons

OTHER NAVIGATION METHODS

Stars, shadows, and more Even without a compass, it is possible to determine direction. The Sun, Moon, and stars are signposts if you know how to read them. There are also clues in the living world.

CELESTIAL NAVIGATION

North To find Polaris, the north polar star, first locate the pattern of stars known as the Plough or Big Dipper. The two bright stars at the end of the Dipper's bowl point to Polaris in the constellation Ursa Minor.

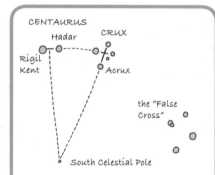

South Draw an imaginary line between the "pointer stars" (Rigil Kent and Hadar). The point where this line intersects with a line extended from the long axis of the Southern Cross (Crux) is the celestial south pole.

LUNAR METHOD

Moonlight guide Imagine a line connecting the horns of the crescent Moon and project it to the horizon. This point indicates approximate south (northern hemisphere) or north (southern hemisphere).

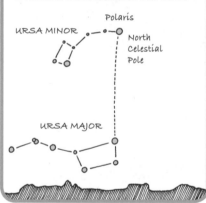

WATCH METHOD

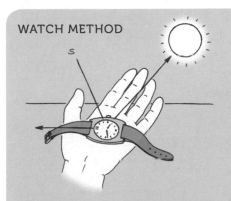

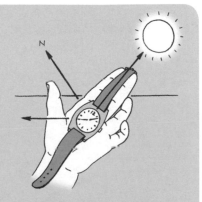

Northern hemisphere Point the hour hand at the Sun. Bisect the angle between the hour hand and the 12 mark to find south.

Southern hemisphere Point the 12 mark at the Sun. Bisect the angle between the hour hand and the 12 mark to find north.

SHADOW TIP METHOD

1 Place a stick vertically in the ground. Mark the shadow's tip with a pebble or some other marker.

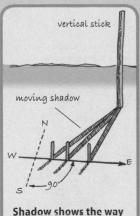

vertical stick

moving shadow

Shadow shows the way
The shadow tip method works in either hemisphere and is most accurate around solar noon.

2 Wait at least ten minutes before marking the shadow's tip with a second marker.

3 The first mark will be on the west side. A line perpendicular to the east–west line will indicate north and south.

LOCATION WITH MAP

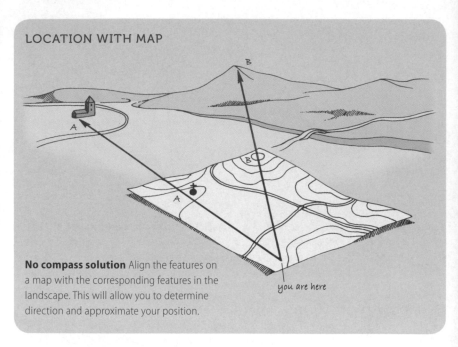

No compass solution Align the features on a map with the corresponding features in the landscape. This will allow you to determine direction and approximate your position.

you are here

NIGHT STAR METHOD

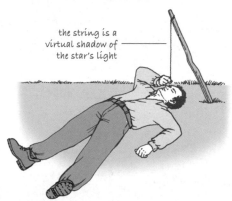

the string is a virtual shadow of the star's light

mark the position with a stick or stone

1 Set a long stick into the ground at a slight angle. Tie a length of string to the end of the stick. Lie on your back, place the string by your temple, and align it with a prominent star.

2 Mark the star's position twice. The first mark will be west and the second will be east. This method works on the same principle as the shadow tip method on the previous page.

SIGNS IN NATURE

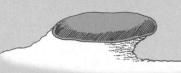

Snow Snowmelt on one side of a tree will indicate south in the northern hemisphere.

Glacial boulder These large rocks sit on pedestals of ice that erode on the south side in the northern hemisphere.

Green sign Moss usually grows better on the shady side of a tree trunk—that's the north side in the northern hemisphere.

Magnetic termites These Australian termites build their mounds aligned north–south to minimize exposure to the Sun.

Travelers palm The leaves of this palm form a dramatic fan that is usually aligned east–west.

PREVAILING WIND

Spider web Do you know which way the wind tends to blow? Spiders do too and will orient their webs sideways to the prevailing wind.

Tree Windswept trees are another good indicator of prevailing winds, and will show you the way if you know the local weather.

DANGERS AND EMERGENCIES

Often when things go wrong in the outdoors, there is no one to call on for help—self-reliance is a must. The greatest tools at your disposal are a positive attitude, the right gear, and a wealth of knowledge.

Signaling

Ground-to-air signaling In an emergency in the wilderness, your first contact with the outside world is likely to be a search aircraft. Make this contact count by knowing standard ground-to-air signals.

GROUND-TO-AIR SIGNALS

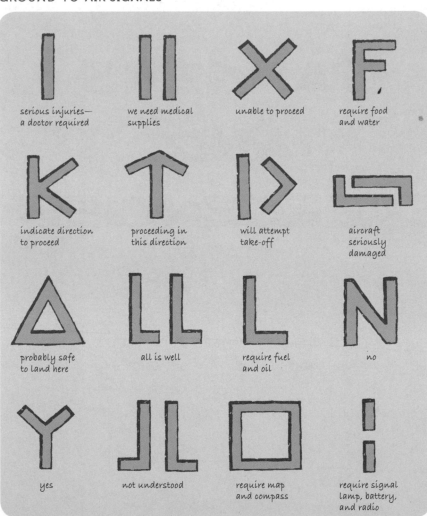

serious injuries— a doctor required

we need medical supplies

unable to proceed

require food and water

indicate direction to proceed

proceeding in this direction

will attempt take-off

aircraft seriously damaged

probably safe to land here

all is well

require fuel and oil

no

yes

not understood

require map and compass

require signal lamp, battery, and radio

BODY SIGNALS

all is well

pick us up

can proceed shortly

need mechanical help

have radio

do NOT attempt to land here

need medical assistance

land here

use drop message

negative

affirmative

Fire cone Keep these fire signals primed with plenty of dry fuel, and ready to go at all times.

Smoke cone During daylight hours, smoke will mark your position more clearly than fire. Surround a fuel source with green branches, rubber, and other materials that will smoke when burned.

Life rafts Three of anything is an internationally recognized distress signal. In thick jungle, the only clear area may be a river. Tether three rafts with fuel for a jungle distress signal.

SMOKE FLARE

flare smoke is usually red or orange and can be seen up to 3 miles away

end cap with pull cord firing mechanism

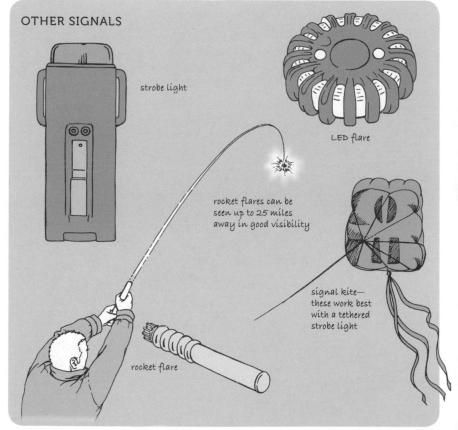

OTHER SIGNALS

strobe light

LED flare

rocket flares can be seen up to 25 miles away in good visibility

signal kite— these work best with a tethered strobe light

rocket flare

SIGNAL MIRROR

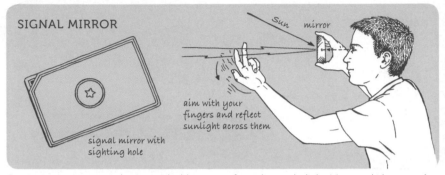

signal mirror with sighting hole

aim with your fingers and reflect sunlight across them

Beam me up A mirror is the most valuable means of signaling in daylight. It's a good idea to pack a signaling mirror if going off the beaten track.

PERSONAL LOCATOR BEACONS

High-tech Personal Locator Beacons (PLBs) are small, lightweight devices that can be activated in an emergency anywhere in the world. They are not cheap, but they can be hired for those times you are in the wilderness or at sea.

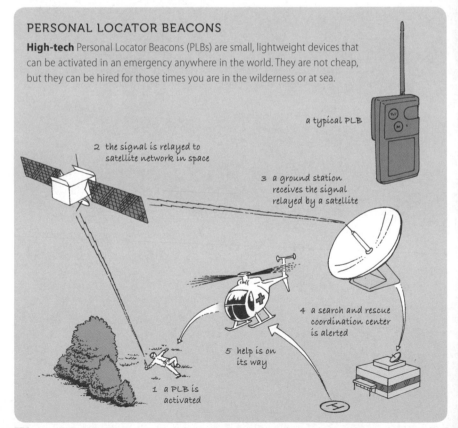

a typical PLB

2 the signal is relayed to satellite network in space

3 a ground station receives the signal relayed by a satellite

4 a search and rescue coordination center is alerted

5 help is on its way

1 a PLB is activated

AIRCRAFT SIGNALS

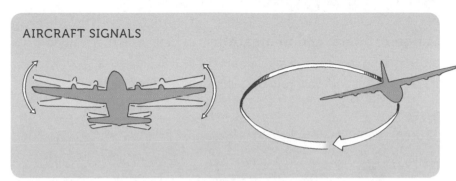

Rocking wings This action indicates that the pilot has seen you or understands your message.

Complete right turn This maneuver indicates that your signal is not understood.

PREPARE A HELICOPTER LANDING ZONE

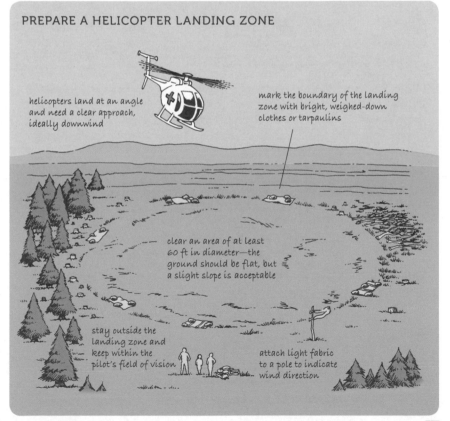

helicopters land at an angle and need a clear approach, ideally downwind

mark the boundary of the landing zone with bright, weighed-down clothes or tarpaulins

clear an area of at least 60 ft in diameter—the ground should be flat, but a slight slope is acceptable

stay outside the landing zone and keep within the pilot's field of vision

attach light fabric to a pole to indicate wind direction

DANGEROUS ANIMALS

Stingers, biters, and maneaters At most times, most creatures will do everything they can to avoid human contact. But it pays to know what species to avoid and what your defenses are when under attack.

INSECTS

Bee A bee sting is painful but is only life-threatening to those who are allergic to them. If you are attacked by a swarm of angry bees, run as fast as possible from the point of first contact, protect your face, and seek shelter.

Ant Ant stings range from innocuous to agonizing. Be sure to avoid the bullet ant (*Paraponera clavata*) of Central and South America. Its sting is considered the most painful of any bee, wasp, or ant.

Wasps and hornets These relatives of bees and ants can sting repeatedly. They can be aggressive when seeking out food and are attracted to sugar and sweet odors. Keep well clear of wasp nests. Allergic reactions can be fatal.

Mosquito The humble mosquito is the deadliest creature on Earth. Mosquito-borne diseases are a particular problem in the tropics, but can occur in temperate regions as well.

Flea A flea bite is normally just an irritation, but they can lead to viral, bacterial, and parasitical diseases, including Lyme disease and bubonic plague. It is prudent to consider any flea as potentially dangerous.

Tsetse fly These large blood-sucking flies are endemic to mid-continental Africa between the Sahara and the Kalahari deserts. They carry the parasite that causes sleeping sickness, which is fatal without treatment.

BOTFLY

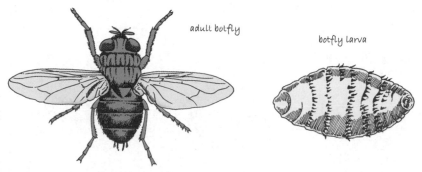

adult botfly

botfly larva

Botfly An egg of the human botfly (*Dermatobia hominis*, native to Mexico, Central, and South America) hatches when it detects human warmth. The larva then burrows into the skin where it grows for about eight weeks. They may cause painful pustules but are otherwise harmless.

REMOVE A BOTFLY LARVAE

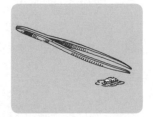

Suffocate The larva needs to breathe. Suffocate it with duct tape or petroleum jelly.

Grasp Apply pressure around the infestation point and pinch the larva tail when it emerges.

Remove Pull steadily until the larva is completely out. Clean and bandage the wound.

CENTIPEDE

Centipedes, especially the larger species, can inflict a painful, venomous bite. If bitten, clean the wound and take painkillers. Be alert to signs of allergic reaction.

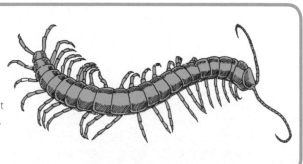

ARACHNIDS

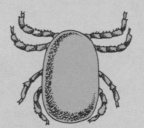

Hard tick These diminutive bloodsucking arachnids are responsible for the spread of numerous viral, bacterial, and protozoan illnesses. The hard tick family (Ixodidae) comprises the majority of tick species. They have a hard shield-like scutum just behind the mouthparts.

Soft tick The less commonly encountered soft ticks (Argasidae) have a rounded, leathery appearance with mouthparts that are not visible from above. These ticks prefer to feed on birds and small mammals, but will choose human hosts if the opportunity presents itself.

Tick removal
Using thin tweezers, grasp the tick as close to the skin as possible and pull upward with a steady even pressure. Do not squeeze the body of the tick—this is likely to cause infection.

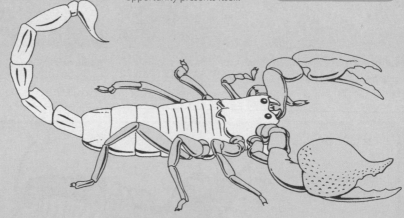

Scorpion About 25 species of scorpions can kill. These inhabit northern Africa, the Middle East, India, Mexico, and parts of South America. Most of the other 1,000 or so species can deliver a very painful sting. Scorpions hide in clothing, boots, and bedding, so shake these out thoroughly before use if you are in scorpion territory.

Funnel-web spider There are about 40 species of funnel-web spiders in Australia. The highly venomous Sydney funnel web spider (*Atrax robustus*) is possibly the world's most dangerous spider. It will strike repeatedly with little provocation.

Widow spider Many spiders of the genus *Latrodectus* are highly venomous. Well-known species include the black widow (North America), the redback spider (Australia), and button spiders (southern Africa). Bites can be fatal without medical intervention.

Brazilian wandering spider This genus of aggressive spiders is found in Central and South America and in banana shipments worldwide. Their venom is the most toxic of any spider.

Tarantula These frightening-looking spiders are actually quite timid. Most bites are comparable to a wasp sting, although one species (*Pelinobius muticus*) causes strong hallucinations. Some species defend themselves by shedding highly irritating hairs.

Recluse spider Bites from these spiders (*Loxosceles* genus) can result in necrotic tissue death requiring skin grafts and other surgical intervention. However, mild lesions and itchiness are the more common consequence.

Copperhead These well-camouflaged North American snakes will often "freeze" when feeling threatened. Consequently, bites often result when they are unwittingly stepped on. Bites are rarely fatal.

Rattlesnake These snakes are responsible for the great majority of snake injuries and deaths in North America (even so, fatalities are very rare). Despite their fearsome reputation, all rattlesnake species are timid. They will normally give a warning rattle when alarmed.

Bushmaster This genus of large venomous vipers is found in remote forested areas of Central and South America. This snake is capable of repeated strikes and the injection of large amounts of venom.

Cottonmouth This semi-aquatic viper (*Agkistrodon piscivorus*) is native to the southeastern United States. A cottonmouth will vibrate its tail and throw its mouth open as a threat display. Bites are painful and potentially fatal.

Coral snake There are over 65 recognized species of coral snakes in the Americas. They have very potent venom, but because of their docile nature and small fangs, deaths and injuries are rare. Many harmless snakes mimic the coral snakes' coloration for protection.

SNAKES—EUROPE

Adder The common adder (*Viper berus*) is the only poisonous snake of northern Europe. It is widespread in densely populated areas, and bites are fairly common but very rarely fatal. Children, the elderly, and infirm are at particular risk. The common adder has several larger and more dangerous relatives in southern Europe.

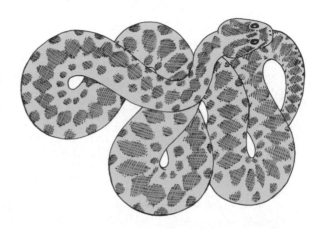

SNAKES—AFRICA AND ASIA

Boomslang The venom of this sub-Saharan snake (*Dispholidus typus*) works as a hemotoxin—even small amounts will cause severe internal and external hemorrhaging. Will strike fast if molested.

Krait This genus of snakes is found in the jungles of India and Southeast Asia. They are armed with a highly toxic neurotoxin that induces muscle paralysis. Without rapid medical intervention, bites tend to be fatal.

Cobra Most cobra species rear up and spread their necks in a threat display. Some can "spit" venom up to eight feet. They aim for the eyes and are generally accurate. A direct hit causes severe burning pain.

SNAKES—AFRICA AND ASIA CONTINUED

Saw scaled viper These small snakes (family *Viperidae*) inhabit dry savanna habitats. They produce a rasping sound when alarmed by rubbing the sides of their bodies together. They are very dangerous.

Puff adder This snake species (*Bitis arietans*) is responsible for more snake bite deaths in Africa than any other. When approached, it draws its head close to its coils, makes a loud hissing sound, and is quick to strike.

Mamba Most mamba species (genus *Dendroaspis*) are tree dwelling. The exception is the terrestrial black mamba which is the world's fastest and Africa's deadliest snake. Untreated, its bite has a fatality rate of 100 percent.

SNAKES—AUSTRALIA

Red-bellied black This snake species (*Pseudechis porphyriacus*) is commonly encountered in woodlands, forests, swamplands, and urban areas of eastern Australia. They are usually reluctant to attack and prefer to escape perceived threats. Bites are dangerous but rarely fatal.

Eastern brown snake The eastern brown snake (*Pseudonaja textilis*) is the species responsible for most deaths caused by snakebite in Australia. Its venom is the most toxic of any land snake in the world, except for the inland taipan (see opposite).

SNAKES—AUSTRALIA CONTINUED

Taipan All species in this genus are dangerous. The inland taipan (*Oxyuranus microlepidotus*) is regarded as the most venomous land snake in the world. However its range is sparsely inhabited and all bite victims have been successfully treated with antivenom.

Tiger snake The common tiger snake (*Notechis scutatus*) is found in southern and eastern Australia. Their highly toxic venom is produced in large amounts. The venom mainly affects the central nervous system, but also causes muscle damage, and affects blood clotting.

Death adder Death adders (genus *Acanthophis*) are found in most parts of Australia, New Guinea, and adjacent islands. They have relatively large fangs and toxic venom. Before the introduction of antivenom, about 60 percent of bites to humans were fatal.

SEA SNAKES

Hydrophiinae Sea snakes are found in warm coastal waters from the Indian Ocean to the Pacific. Some species have venom more toxic than any land snake. Sea snakes are curious and will readily approach divers and swimmers, but they are generally placid and harmless to humans if left in peace.

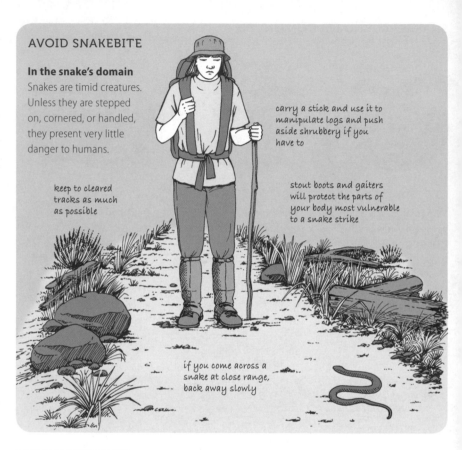

AVOID SNAKEBITE

In the snake's domain
Snakes are timid creatures. Unless they are stepped on, cornered, or handled, they present very little danger to humans.

carry a stick and use it to manipulate logs and push aside shrubbery if you have to

keep to cleared tracks as much as possible

stout boots and gaiters will protect the parts of your body most vulnerable to a snake strike

if you come across a snake at close range, back away slowly

TREAT SNAKEBITE

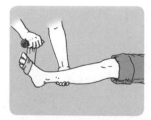

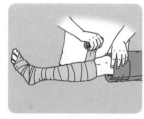

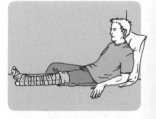

1 Snake bites usually occur on a limb. Start applying a pressure bandage just above the toes or fingers.

2 Continue as far up the limb as possible. This retards the movement of the venom and the onset of symptoms.

3 Apply a splint to the limb and keep it below the level of the heart. Keep the victim calm and monitor his breathing.

OTHER REPTILES

Gila monster This species (*Heloderma suspectum*) of venomous lizard is native to the southwestern United States and the northwestern Mexican state of Sonora. Although a Gila bite is extremely painful, none has resulted in a confirmed human death.

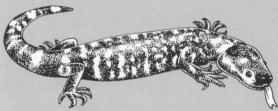

Beaded lizard A close relative of the Gila monster, the beaded lizard is found principally in Mexico and southern Guatemala. Its bite causes excruciating pain, swelling, and a rapid drop in blood pressure.

Crocodile Two crocodile species—the Nile crocodile (*Crocodylus niloticus*) and the saltwater crocodile (*Crocodylus porosus*)—are notorious maneaters. Stay well away from water where crocodiles are known to be present.

Alligator The American alligator (*Alligator mississippiensis*) is native to the southeastern United States. Alligators are generally wary of humans but will occasionally attack unprovoked. Alligator bites frequently result in dangerous infections.

AQUATIC ANIMALS (FRESHWATER)

Piranha The mouths of these South American freshwater river fish (family *Characidae*) are packed with sharp triangular teeth designed to puncture and rip flesh. While they will not strip humans to the bone, piranhas will take isolated bites of flesh and remove toes.

Candiru The Amazon's most feared fish (family *Trichomycteridae*) usually survives by invading the gills of larger fish, where it feeds on blood. However, it has been known to lodge itself in the human urethra instead. Play it safe and never urinate while submerged in the Amazon.

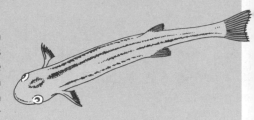

Bull shark This shark species (*Carcharhinus leucas*) survives happily in the open ocean and hundreds of miles up rivers. Because of their wide distribution and aggression, many experts consider them the most dangerous sharks in the world.

Electric eel When angry, these large South American fish (*Electrophorus electricus*) can deliver a burst of 600 volts—more than enough to kill. However, such deaths are very rare, suggesting they need severe provocation before attacking.

AQUATIC ANIMALS (ESTUARINE AND OCEAN)

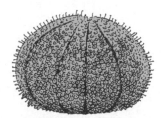

Flower urchin Many sea urchins are armed with sharp spines and should be avoided. The spines of a flower urchin (*Toxopneustes pileolus*) inject an extremely toxic venom. Injuries are very painful, and deaths have been reported.

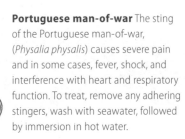

Box jellyfish These deadly jellyfish (*Chironex fleckeri*) live in coastal waters off northern Australia and throughout the Indo-Pacific. A box jellyfish sting is so excruciating and overwhelming that a victim can immediately go into shock and drown if swimming alone. Cardiac arrest often follows swiftly.

Portuguese man-of-war The sting of the Portuguese man-of-war, (*Physalia physalis*) causes severe pain and in some cases, fever, shock, and interference with heart and respiratory function. To treat, remove any adhering stingers, wash with seawater, followed by immersion in hot water.

Cone shell These pretty marine snails (genus *Conus*) prey upon other marine organisms, immobilizing them with unique venoms. A sting from a large cone shell brings severe pain and is potentially fatal. Treat as with a snakebite. There is no antivenom.

AQUATIC ANIMALS (ESTUARINE AND OCEAN)

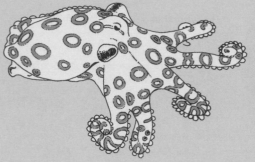

Blue-ringed octopus These octopus (genus *Hapalochlaena*) live in tide pools in the Pacific Ocean from Japan to Australia. Although small and docile, they carry enough venom to kill 26 adults within minutes. Stings can bring total paralysis without loss of consciousness. Victims require artificial respiration for survival.

Needle fish These shallow marine-dwelling fish (family *Belonidae*) make short jumps out of the water at speeds up to 40 miles per hour. Their sharp beaks can inflict deep puncture wounds and often break off inside the victim. They are particularly excited by artificial light at night.

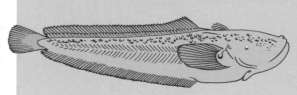

Toadfish Venomous toadfish (family *Batrachoididae*) occur in tropical waters off the coasts of Central and South America. They have sharp, very poisonous spines hidden in their dorsal fins. They bury themselves in the sand and are easily stepped on.

Stonefish These inhabitants (family *Synanceiidae*) of coastal waters of the tropical Indo-Pacific are the world's most venomous fish. Symptoms of the venom are muscle weakness, temporary paralysis, and shock, which may result in death if not treated.

Shark Although greatly feared, shark attacks on humans are extremely rare. No shark is thought to target humans as prey, and only four species have been involved in a significant number of fatal, unprovoked attacks on humans.

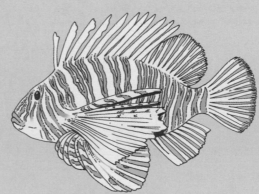

Lionfish This genus (*Pterois*) of aggressive territorial fish is native to the tropical Indo-Pacific and has been introduced into the Atlantic coastal waters of the United States. Pterois venom can result in vomiting, fever, and sweating, and has been lethal in a few cases.

Stingray These docile fish (order *Myliobatiformes*) are equipped with a venomous barbed sting on the tail. People are usually stung when they accidentally step on a stingray. Stings can result in local trauma, pain, swelling, nausea, and muscle cramps.

MAMMALS

American black bear
These medium-sized bears (*Ursus americanus*) rarely attack humans. Avoid contact if possible, and fight back if attacked. The most dangerous black bears are those that are hungry or have become habituated to human contact.

front track

hind track

Brown bear These large bears (*Ursus arctos*) are normally unpredictable in temperament, and will attack if they are surprised or feel threatened. Mothers with cubs are particularly dangerous. If attacked, protect the back of the neck and play dead.

hind track

front track

bear repellent spray

Polar bear Contact with the world's largest land carnivore (*Ursus maritimus*) should be avoided. A well-fed polar bear normally avoids people or may show signs of curiosity. A hungry bear may stalk, kill, and eat you. The best defense against a polar bear attack is a high-powered rifle. Failing that, curl up in a ball and play dead.

front track

hind track

Vampire bat

The common vampire bat (*Desmodus rotundus*) is native to the American tropics and subtropics. They will feed on human blood when horse and cattle are in short supply. Bites can cause rabies—a deadly viral infection.

Bull There is nothing like a large bull (*Bos taurus*) to turn a pleasant walk through the countryside into a frightening ordeal. Never turn your back on a bull that has its head lowered or is pawing the ground. Back away slowly. Withdrawing about 20 feet can avert the dangerous behavior.

Hippopotamus

The hippopotamus (*Hippopotamus amphibius*) is responsible for more human fatalities in Africa than any other large animal. They are extremely aggressive, unpredictable, and unafraid of humans.

Rhinoceros The five extant species of rhinoceros (family Rhinocerotidae) are known for charging with no provocation. With very poor eyesight, they are inclined to panic at strange smells and sounds.

Tiger The tiger (*Panthera tigris*) is the largest of the cat species. Humans appear to be a prey of last resort for tigers, but individual maneaters have been responsible for hundreds of deaths.

Lion As with tigers, humans are not a favored prey of lions (*Panthera leo*). However, where human habitation encroaches on lion territory and regular prey animals are in short supply, lions will hunt and kill humans.

Leopard Attacks by leopards (*Panthera pardus*) on humans are rare, however injured, sick, or struggling individuals may turn to human flesh. The "Leopard of Panar" is reported to have killed as many as 400 people in northern India in the early years of the 20th century.

Wolf Like any large predator, a wolf (*Canis lupus*) is potentially dangerous, and common sense demands we seek to avoid them. Fortunately, attacks on people are very rare. Rabid wolves in the "furious" stage are the most dangerous.

DANGEROUS PLANTS

Mean and green Plants have evolved a range of effective deterrents against animals that might want to eat them. Some need just the lightest touch and you're in trouble.

Stinging nettle This herbaceous plant (*Urtica dioica*) is common in many temperate parts of the world. Hairs on the leaves and stems contain irritating chemicals, which are released when the plant comes in contact with the skin.

the stinging hairs

Cacti Large cactus spines can be removed with tweezers. Take care and work slowly because some spines have barbed ends. To remove very small, fine spines, apply duct tape to the affected area, then gently remove it.

poison sumac

poison ivy

poison oak

Poison ivy, poison oak, and poison sumac These related plants grow plentifully in parts of the United States and southern Canada. While people vary greatly in their sensitivity to these plants, most people who touch them will be affected by rashes and blistering.

Stinging trees There are about 37 species of stinging trees distributed across Southeast Asia, Australia, and the Pacific Islands. Avoid at all costs Australian Gympie-Gympie (*Dendrocnide moroides*)—one touch can mean months of agonizing pain.

QUICKSAND

That sinking feeling Quicksand is a mass of fine sand, silt, and clay that is supersaturated with water. While it's hard to get out of, quicksand won't inexorably suck you under the way it does in the movies.

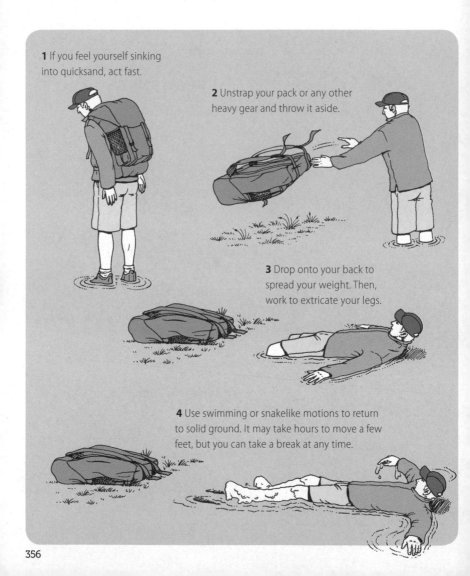

1 If you feel yourself sinking into quicksand, act fast.

2 Unstrap your pack or any other heavy gear and throw it aside.

3 Drop onto your back to spread your weight. Then, work to extricate your legs.

4 Use swimming or snakelike motions to return to solid ground. It may take hours to move a few feet, but you can take a break at any time.

SOURCING WATER

The first priority If you are lost or your supplies are exhausted, your first priority should be to find water. In some settings, water is abundant, but in arid areas, this can be a life-or-death challenge.

ANIMAL INDICATORS

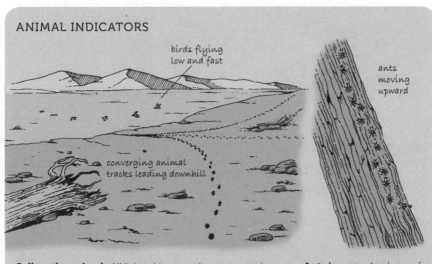

birds flying low and fast

ants moving upward

converging animal tracks leading downhill

Follow the animals All living things need water to survive. Observe the animals in your surroundings and you will get valuable clues. Don't forget plants. Unusually green plants in an arid landscape may indicate water just below the surface.

Ants in a row A column of ants heading up a tree trunk may be heading to a reservoir of water.

DISTANCE TO WATER

Bees Usually within 3 miles.

Flies Usually within 1.5 miles.

Mosquitoes Usually within 1,500 feet.

Frogs Usually in the immediate vicinity.

DRY RIVERBED

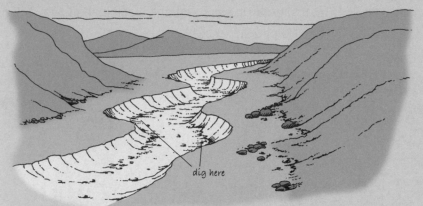

dig here

Watercourse In a waterless landscape, a dry, sandy riverbed is often the best place to look for water. The best places to dig are the lowest points, the outside of bends, and anywhere that green plants are growing. You may need to dig down three feet or more before striking water.

CLIFF BASE

dig here

dig here

Go where the water goes Water naturally pools at the base of cliffs and hills. Such pools are deep and often the last to disappear because they are protected or partially protected from the sun. If no water is found, dig in places where it would pool after rain.

BEACH

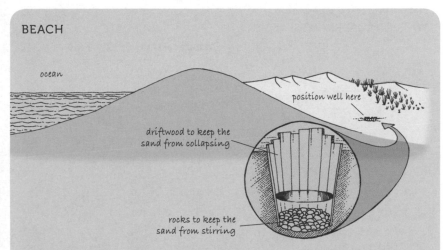

ocean

position well here

driftwood to keep the
sand from collapsing

rocks to keep the
sand from stirring

Beach well A beach well is just a hole, dug behind the very first sand dune in from the ocean. It should be about three feet deep. Fresh groundwater seeping toward the ocean will accumulate in the well and float on top of the salty seawater.

UNSAFE WATER

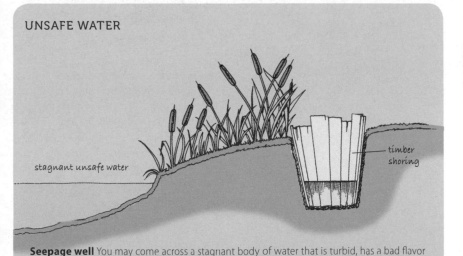

stagnant unsafe water

timber
shoring

Seepage well You may come across a stagnant body of water that is turbid, has a bad flavor or odor, or is simply difficult to access. In these circumstances dig a well about ten feet from the water source. The water that fills the well will be filtered and should be safe to drink.

WATER FROM PLANTS

machete

Green coconut Slice open a green coconut with a sharp knife to access the water inside. Drink the coconut water in moderation because it is a natural laxative.

Mature coconut Use a sharpened stake driven into the ground to split and remove the fibrous outer husk and reveal the shell. Drive a hole through a soft "eye" of the shell to access the coconut water.

stake

coconut husks

banana tree

cut here

Banana tree Cut through the trunk of a banana tree about four inches above the ground. Then, hollow out a bowl-like reservoir inside the stump. Water from the roots will accumulate in the bowl. At first, the water will be bitter. Scoop the water out of the bowl three times before drinking.

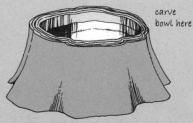

carve bowl here

Green bamboo Green bamboo can supply you with fresh water, even at the height of the tropical dry season. To collect water from a young stalk, bend it over, tie it securely, and cut off the top. Water will drip out of the cut. Collect it in a container.

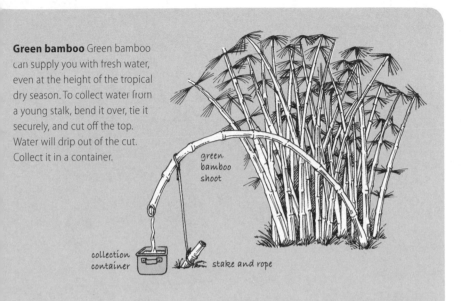

green bamboo shoot

collection container

stake and rope

make two 45° angle cuts

Water from a vine Cut a section of a vine high up. Then, sever it completely near the ground. Liquid will drain out the bottom. Don't drink from vines that produce white sap or milky liquid when cut. Discard liquid with a sour or bitter taste.

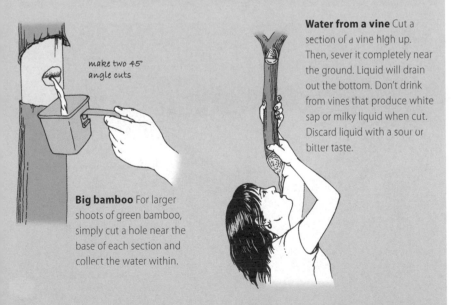

Big bamboo For larger shoots of green bamboo, simply cut a hole near the base of each section and collect the water within.

TRANSPIRATION

Transpiration bag
This is one of the most efficient and easily constructed sources of water in an arid setting. Tie a plastic bag around a leafy branch of a medium-sized tree or shrub. After a few hours in the sun, you will have a cup or so of clean, drinkable water.

rock weight

SOLAR STILL

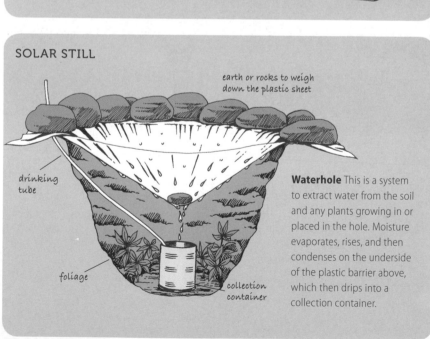

earth or rocks to weigh down the plastic sheet

drinking tube

foliage

collection container

Waterhole This is a system to extract water from the soil and any plants growing in or placed in the hole. Moisture evaporates, rises, and then condenses on the underside of the plastic barrier above, which then drips into a collection container.

WATER FROM CUTTINGS

Cut and dried Collect as many green leaves and branches as can fit in a plastic bag without touching the sides. Prop up the center to form a tent. Arrange the bag on a slight slope so the condensation will run down to a collection point.

padded stick

green cuttings

rocks to keep the vegetation elevated

TRANSPIRATION ON THE GROUND

Ground level This arrangement works on the same principle as the transpiration bag opposite, but with plants that grow close to the ground. Consider scaling up from a plastic bag by using the fly of a tent.

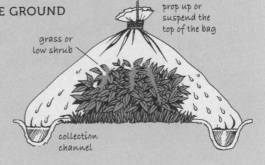

prop up or suspend the top of the bag

grass or low shrub

collection channel

CACTI

Spiky saviors Cacti are a valuable survival resource in many deserts. The fruits of the prickly pear and some other species are edible. Many cacti contain huge amounts of water in their flesh that can be harvested in solar stills or transpiration bags. Note that cacti are protected species in some areas and should be exploited only in an emergency.

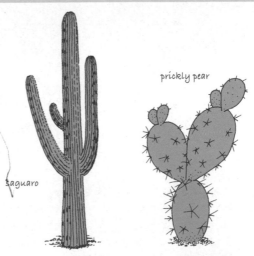

prickly pear

saguaro

WATER PURIFICATION

Keep it clean In the wild, even water that looks pure and pristine may not be. Fortunately, having clean drinking water is relatively simple when you have the right equipment and knowledge.

boiling vessel

condensation vessel

Distill This system is trickier than simple boiling, but it provides pure, drinkable water from sources heavy with sediment. It can also be used to distill seawater or urine.

Boil This kills most types of disease-causing organisms. Boil the water vigorously for at least one minute, then let it cool.

water treatment tablets can be bought from camping stores

Chemical Iodine, potassium permanganate, and chlorine can be used to treat water. They take time to work—and be prepared for a slightly odd taste.

Solar Pour suspect water into clear plastic PET bottles and expose them to direct sunlight for at least six hours (or for two days in very cloudy conditions).

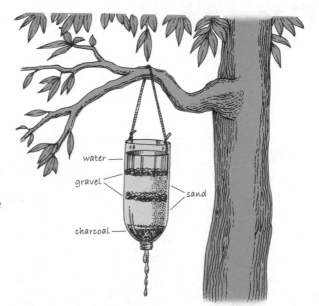

Filter Thorough water filtration is effective at removing particles and many pathogens, but it's still a good idea to boil the water before drinking it.

water
gravel
sand
charcoal

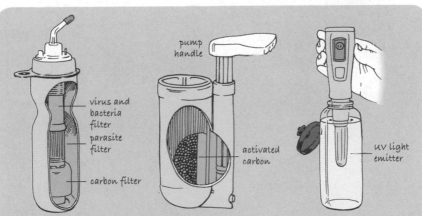

virus and bacteria filter
parasite filter
carbon filter

pump handle

activated carbon

uv light emitter

Bottle filter This filter bottle works with a cartridge that needs to be replaced after every 160 refills, or 26 gallons of water. Simply squeeze to produce a flow of water.

Pump filter There are numerous pump filtration systems on the market for hikers. Each stroke of the pump draws suspect water through the filter and purifies it.

Ultraviolet This handy battery-driven device uses ultraviolet light to sterilize 33 ounces of water in 90 seconds. The water must be clear for the sterilization to work well.

FOOD FROM PLANTS

Plants for life So you're stuck in the wilderness, and you've got sufficient safe drinking water? Your next priorities will probably be food and shelter. Plants can provide abundant nutrition if you know what's safe to eat.

EDIBILITY TEST

1 Crush and smell the plant sample. Reject it if you detect strong, acid, or almond odors.

2 Crush and rub the sample against the inside of your elbow. Wait 15 minutes. Reject if there is any irritation.

Split Separate the plant into its basic components and test separately.

flowers

leaves

stems

roots

3 Hold a small amount against the lips. Reject if there is any irritation.

4 Place a small amount on the tongue. Reject if there is any bad taste or irritation.

5 Chew a small amount for several minutes, but do not swallow.

All clear? If the plant part passes all these tests, consume a small amount and wait several hours for any adverse reaction.

PLANTS TO AVOID

Warning signs Some plants should be avoided altogether. Look for these indicators and leave them be.

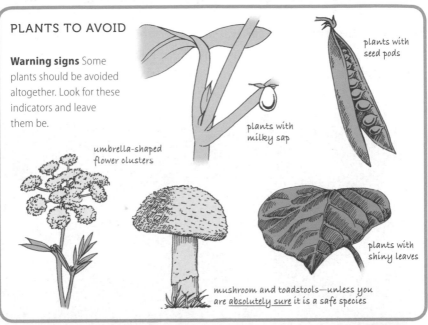

plants with seed pods

plants with milky sap

umbrella-shaped flower clusters

plants with shiny leaves

mushroom and toadstools—unless you are <u>absolutely sure</u> it is a safe species

PLANTS TO EAT?

Watch the wildlife Most foods consumed by primates and birds are safe for us to eat, too. But this is not a guarantee— use the edibility test opposite.

Berry good About 90 percent of aggregate berries are safe to eat.

HUNTING SMALL GAME

Meat on the menu In a survival situation, a meal of meat goes a lot further than plants alone. While large animals can be difficult and dangerous to hunt, their smaller relatives can be on your plate with comparative ease.

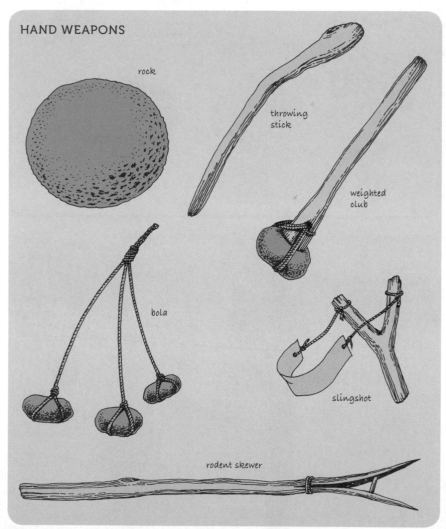

HAND WEAPONS

rock

throwing stick

weighted club

bola

slingshot

rodent skewer

Wriggle and snatch Hold one hand about two feet in front of the frog and slowly wriggle your fingers. This will monopolize the frog's attention. Grab the frog from behind with your other hand.

Lizard lasso Gently wave a noose of tight wire in front of the lizard. Gradually bring the noose closer and closer, then lasso the lizard.

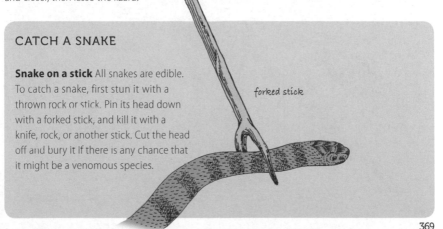

CATCH A SNAKE

Snake on a stick All snakes are edible. To catch a snake, first stun it with a thrown rock or stick. Pin its head down with a forked stick, and kill it with a knife, rock, or another stick. Cut the head off and bury it if there is any chance that it might be a venomous species.

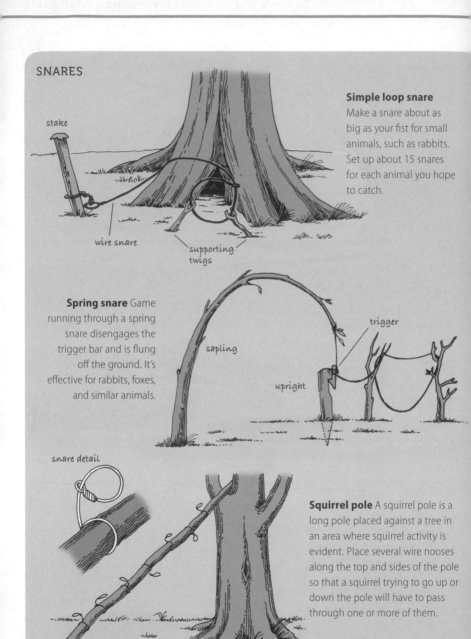

SNARES

stake

wire snare

supporting twigs

Simple loop snare
Make a snare about as big as your fist for small animals, such as rabbits. Set up about 15 snares for each animal you hope to catch.

Spring snare Game running through a spring snare disengages the trigger bar and is flung off the ground. It's effective for rabbits, foxes, and similar animals.

sapling

upright

trigger

snare detail

Squirrel pole A squirrel pole is a long pole placed against a tree in an area where squirrel activity is evident. Place several wire nooses along the top and sides of the pole so that a squirrel trying to go up or down the pole will have to pass through one or more of them.

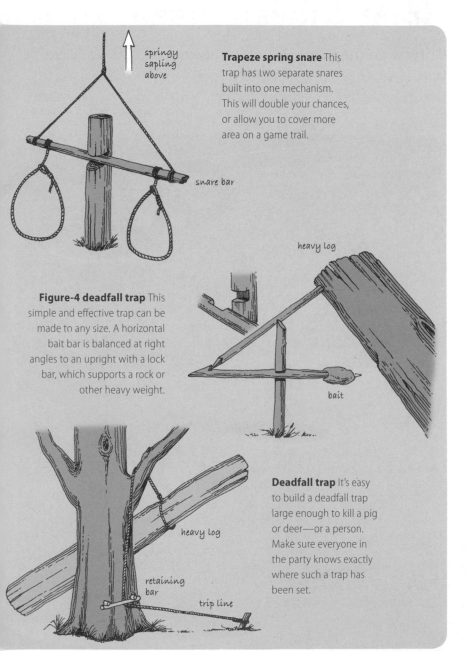

Trapeze spring snare This trap has two separate snares built into one mechanism. This will double your chances, or allow you to cover more area on a game trail.

springy sapling above

snare bar

heavy log

Figure-4 deadfall trap This simple and effective trap can be made to any size. A horizontal bait bar is balanced at right angles to an upright with a lock bar, which supports a rock or other heavy weight.

bait

Deadfall trap It's easy to build a deadfall trap large enough to kill a pig or deer—or a person. Make sure everyone in the party knows exactly where such a trap has been set.

heavy log

retaining bar

trip line

EDIBLE INVERTEBRATES

Critters on the menu Not only can insects, mollusks, and arachnids be found in large quantities, but they are highly nutritious, being rich in fats, proteins, and carbohydrates. If survival is at stake, put your prejudices aside.

Worms There are few better sources of protein than worms. Drop them in potable water after collection and they will purge themselves. If you prefer, dry and grind the worms and add them to soup.

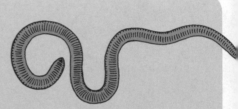

Snails Before eating them, starve snails for a few days so they can excrete any poisonous plants they may have been feeding on. Boil snails for three minutes. Drain, rinse in cold water, then remove them from their shells. Avoid snails with brightly colored shells.

Spiders Don't overlook spiders as a source of protein. Eat the bodies and leave the heads, which may contain poison. If you catch a tarantula, try frying it—they are a delicacy in parts of Southeast Asia.

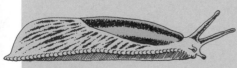

Slugs Some slugs are very large—three or four will constitute a good meal. They can be eaten raw, but are much more appetizing cooked. Prepare and cook them exactly the same way as snails.

Grubs Insect larvae, also known as grubs, are prime wilderness food. They favor cool, damp places, so look in rotten logs, under the bark of dead trees, under rocks, and in the ground. Grubs are safe to eat raw, and delicious cooked.

Grasshoppers These insects can be an abundant source of food in some places. Knock them from the air with a piece of clothing or leafy branch. Remove the wings, antennae, and legs before eating them. It is best to roast them to kill off any parasites.

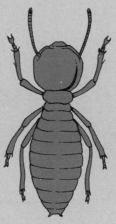

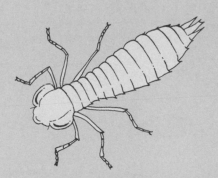

Aquatic insects Nearly all aquatic insects can be eaten in both adult and larval form, and are generally more agreeable than their terrestrial relatives. Use a piece of clothing or other material to act as a net and trawl freshwater rivers or ponds.

Termites These communal insects exist in enormous numbers in the warmer parts of the world and are easily collected from their nests. Remove the wings from larger species before eating. They can be cooked, but are more nutritious eaten raw.

EMERGENCY SHELTERS

Safe and secure Hot or cold, wet or dry, a good shelter is vital for your safety and morale. Each terrain requires different types of shelter. Use the natural resources at hand for the most appropriate version.

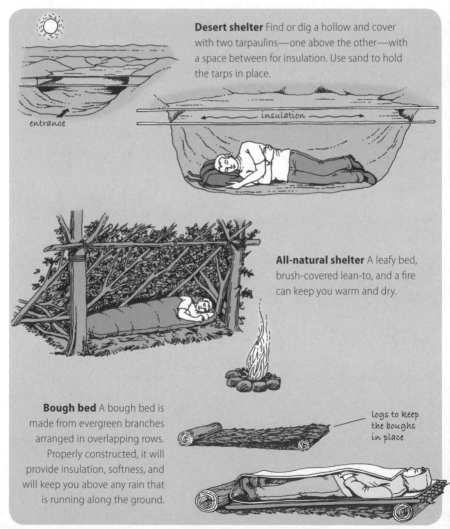

Desert shelter Find or dig a hollow and cover with two tarpaulins—one above the other—with a space between for insulation. Use sand to hold the tarps in place.

entrance

insulation

All-natural shelter A leafy bed, brush-covered lean-to, and a fire can keep you warm and dry.

Bough bed A bough bed is made from evergreen branches arranged in overlapping rows. Properly constructed, it will provide insulation, softness, and will keep you above any rain that is running along the ground.

logs to keep the boughs in place

Fallen tree shelter A fallen tree can make a ready-made shelter. You can improve it by removing branches on the underside and slinging a tarpaulin on top.

check that the broken part is strong enough to last the night

tie the tops together

Sapling shelter If you come across a growth of saplings, clear the ground between them, strip their branches, and lash their tops together. Cover the structure with material or weave branches between them.

weigh down the covering

shore up the "roof" with extra branches

Tree pit snow shelter In forests where heavy snow has fallen, you will often find deep hollows under the branches of evergreen trees. Dig out some extra room if required, and lay some branches on the ground for insulation.

INDEX

THUNDER BAY
P · R · E · S · S

Thunder Bay Press
An imprint of the Baker & Taylor Publishing Group
10350 Barnes Canyon Road, San Diego, CA 92121
www.thunderbaybooks.com

ISBN-13: 978-1-60710-720-0
ISBN-10: 1- 60710-720-1
Library of Congress Cataloging-in-Publication Data available upon request.
Printed in China
1 2 3 4 5 16 15 14 13 12

Illustrations Peter Bull Art Studio

The paper used in the manufacture of this book is sourced from wood
grown in sustainable forests. It complies with the
Environmental Management System Standard ISO 14001:2004